You *Believe*, You *Experience*

The Creative Nature of Thoughts, Meditation, and Foundational Belief Systems

Ronald Lawrence Hays

DEDICATION

For Mama, I love you. And my Toadies- Catherine, Linda, Billie, Roseann, Jennifer and Penny. Thank you all for keeping me right-sized.

ACKNOWLEDGMENTS

Many thanks to Kathleen for your great editing and suggestions. You are the BEST Turtle

CONTENTS

Ronald Lawrence Hays

What Was I Thinking?

I was thinking that this book would be about meditation and the creative nature of thoughts. To a certain degree it will be about those. Ultimately, it will be about beliefs and Belief Systems. And we can't get to these without understanding what comprises them. So, of course meditation and the creative nature of thoughts will be a part of the journey.

First off, I don't have all the answers. Nor do I live with perfect ease and in flawless application of the things that I have written about. Like each of you I am making my way— exploring, hoping, understanding, learning, stumbling, wondering and well LIVING life. The life I am living causes me to be curious and intrigued by my ever-evolving relationship, understanding and experience of God. And how all of that is directly tied to my thoughts and beliefs.

When I was younger, I was under the impression that it was my job to understand this immutable Being referred to as God. That steady, unchanging, omnipotent being could be understood, if I made the effort. As I moved through life this idea was left somewhere in the dust by my EXPERIENCE of God.

At the time I did not describe this as my experience of God, but as my spiritual journey. In my eyes I couldn't get far enough away from the impression of God that had been foisted upon me by culture and society. I thought mine was a journey away from God and toward understanding. Boy was I blind.

My curiosity and desire to leave God behind and discover him elsewhere continues to take me on a journey that began in my heart and mind. The old cliché that it was there all along revealed itself as being so true time and time again.

Much of what I have come to know and believe has been realized in hindsight. Upon reflection, I realized that it was during those times when I slowed down and took notice of where I had been, how I had gotten there and what I experienced that I learned and grew the most; came to know

God a little more. In the midst of a lot of it I was too busy living, too busy surviving, too busy running to know that I was becoming more aware. I was just trying to live.

Like many of you, my teen years were bumpy as hell. In spite of the bumps, I had an innate desire to understand what and who God was in relation to me. I went to every church I could get to. I studied the Bible, read books and latched on to people who seemed to know God. Baptists, Presbyterians, Jehovah Witnesses---you name it and I brushed up against it. I gathered as many ideas about God as I could. But, eventually they each left me feeling dissatisfied and alone, thirsty for more. Something about each set of beliefs just didn't make sense. The rationale and logic behind them was faulty—in my eyes. They did not work when I tried to apply them in my real life.

By the time I was 20 I left my experience of organized Religion behind with a heavy but determined heart. My real journey had begun in earnest. Despite the pitfalls of addiction, life's ups and downs, emotional turbulence and all the usual stuff of life, I had an unquenchable thirst to understand and know my purpose for being, where I fit and who or what fit me there.

It was about this time that I stumbled across creative visualization and several other positive thinking concepts and tools. WOW! I had no idea that I was so powerful; that my thoughts could be controlled and directed. I was thrilled and excited by these new ideas and jumped in headfirst. For the first time in my life I felt empowered by beliefs that were spiritual in nature, but not religious. I continued to stumble through the pitfalls of life, but at times I was able to put these new tools into practice with amazing results.

I could not get enough of books, movies, conversations and experiences that expanded my understanding of Positive Thinking and Visualization. Many of the ideas that I pursued during this time could be lumped into New Age or pop-psychology categories. Bit by bit I was learning how to steer my own ship. Many times I ended up on the rocks.

In my early 30s I met two 'Angels'. One of these Angels was someone whose social skills were less than stellar and honestly it was challenging to be around him. Despite this, we became friends and when we discussed New Thought, spirituality, God and our nature, his social skills became 'right on the money'. Periodically, he would leave books at my doorstep on a variety of spiritual topics. I never knew when or what I would find and I devoured them all. Past lives, aliens, meditation, sojourns and so much more. This went on for a couple of years.

During this time I met another 'Angel' whose presence in my life opened me to even more possibilities and ideas. Through books and hours long conversations and exploration, this friend fanned the desire I had for more understanding, and possibilities. I didn't always agree with her perspectives, but there was always something that I wanted to hold onto. I was bursting at the seams with excitement.

This is not to say that my life was perfect with this influx of ideas and possibilities. Despite my passion for exploring new ideas and principles I was not always able to apply them in a practical way. I didn't always know what to do with them beyond an intellectual and emotional pursuit.

Finally, the missing component that would help me pull it all together came into my life. This new element removed barriers and allowed me to truly have a conscious relationship with myself and the Divine.

I was in a Yoga class and, as it came to a close, the instructor asked everyone to recline and close their eyes. She moved about the room, took something from a shelf and then I heard the most amazing sound. It went in, around and through me and I suddenly felt as expansive as the Universe. I was no longer in the confines of my body or my mind. After what seemed a lengthy amount of time, I sat up and said, "Where did I go?!"

The sound that I heard was a Quartz Crystal Singing Bowl. In that moment I had an epiphany. Everything that I had read, discussed, explored and sought during the past years suddenly began to coalesce. I experienced MYSELF and GOD in that moment. My nature was no longer just a concept and intellectual wondering---it was an experience. The Bowl had taken me beneath the chatter of my mind. Well, I had to have one! One bowl turned into two. Two turned into three. I started to give them as gifts and eventually I had a small group of friends who would come together and play Bowls, drums and other instruments. Each time I heard and played the Bowls I experienced an altered state of being—in my mind, body and Soul.

For those of you who do not know what Quartz Crystal Signing Bowls are, they are bowls generally ranging in size from 12" to 18" in diameter. They are made of Quartz Crystal and are played like a musical instrument using a mallet. They are played similar to how you might run your finger along the edge of a water glass. The sound they produce is nothing short of AMAZING. It moves in, through and around you. With each bowl being tuned to a different note and tone it is a symphonic effect for mind, body and Soul.

After a period of time, someone suggested that I give a Crystal Bowl concert. I thought, "What the heck?" The concert eventually became a regular event and along the way I began to explore the meditative influence of the Bowls. I started to talk for a few minutes before each event about the creative nature of thoughts and meditation. Finally, I developed exercises and tools to help people take the experience of the Bowls into their daily lives to expand an existing meditation practice or to begin a new one. The event had become a regular EXPERIENCE.

Through my experience with the Bowls, I discovered meditation and the creative nature of my thoughts in a very real and practical way. It was like getting the instruction manual for everything else that was floating around in my head. The experience continues to pull everything together for me.

So came the next part of my ongoing journey. How can I share with others, who desire this type of connection, how to have a similar connection in their own lives? Answering that question is what this book is about—for you and for me.

For Notes, Thoughts and Ponderings

Nothing New

There is nothing new in these pages, which is at the root of everything that I have come to experience as True. *There is nothing new.* Someone has already said it, explored it, explained it or put it forth. Each generation of Spiritual Teachers simply brings Universal Truths through their own filter. I am eternally grateful that the teachers who have influenced me did so. They have changed my life, my experience of myself and my experience of God. Thank You.

So, if there is nothing new here then why read this book? Well, these ideas about the creative nature of thoughts and meditation have become very main-stream in our culture. Imagine that 30 years ago people did not run around saying "I create my reality." There were certainly schools of thought and pockets of people who did acknowledge these Truths.

Today, it is just accepted that we have at least some role in creating our experience in life. That's an amazing paradigm shift and there are many wonderful advantages to the acceptance of these powerful Truths.

Bestselling books, TV shows, movies, websites and conferences are all putting these Truths forth. More people than ever recognize what they think has a direct impact on their health, well-being and quality of life. They have come to know that their thoughts play a powerful and creative role in one's life.

Along with this mainstream exposure and acceptance comes a clichéd view of these Truths as well. We have become so used to hearing them that many of us hardly pay attention anymore. We've read so many books about them that we have become less likely to consciously recognize what this means for us in our daily lives. We say, *"Yeah, I know, my thoughts are creative. I create my reality. Now tell me something that I don't know."*

You Believe, You Experience stops right there and encourages you to ask yourself, *"What do I believe?"* and then *"How do those beliefs create my experiences?"*

How endlessly fascinating and amazing that the beginning of all of your experiences in life happens within the space of your mind? Your thoughts create the foundation for all of your experiences! I for one can spend the rest of my life coming to understand the implications of this. I think you can too.

As we get started, here is what I hope you will gain from reading this book-

- A basic understanding of the creative nature and power of your mind, thoughts and beliefs.

- A set of basic tools to begin or resume the exploration of your internal landscape through meditation and an understanding of how that landscape creates and impacts your outer world.

- The desire to allow all that is presented here to be your starting point for a lifelong journey into awareness of self, others and the greater whole.

There are a lot of ideas out there about God, meditation, spirituality and the creative nature of thoughts and beliefs. There are also just as many ideas out there about how to incorporate those ideas into your life. Someone or some entity will always be willing to step up and tell you why and how. *Suppose you tell yourself why and how?*

You don't have to *believe* (have a collection of thoughts) that God or anything like Him exists to benefit from reading **and** using this book. This journey is about what happens in *your* mind, within the space of *your* own skin and how it all comes together to create your experience of both your inner and outer world. Your belief in God is just one of the many conclusions that you will explore.

In my years of wandering and wondering, I have come to experience that Truths, and the principles that underpin them, are simple. So, my intention is to make everything accessible and practical with the use of every day, conversational language. Not a lot of esoteric rambling and wordy explanations that would just cloud and convolute rather than convey.

OH! One more thing. What would a book of this nature be without tools and exercises? I have read enough of these types of books to know that many of us start out with the best of intentions and after the first page generally skip over the exercises and tools. Right? **PLEASE** make the commitment to try these. You already have the ability to *intellectualize* these TRUTHS. What you need to begin to do is *apply* them; *live them*. It is one thing to know these Truths conceptually, but if you combine that understanding with experience then you will come to know them EXPERIENTIALLY. This is what true knowledge is all about. The tools and exercises will help you begin to know experientially.

Since you are making the commitment to try the exercises and tools, I will commit to make them fun, simple and about 15 minutes a day, to begin with. You will need a timer, a set of highlighters, pen and paper and the willingness to sit quietly for up to 15 minutes.

Recognize that you don't have to travel to far and distant lands to become enlightened. The Eastern is no more mystical than the Western; the urban no less close to God than the Rural. No place on the planet is more sacred than any other. This would imply that there is some place that the Divine is not or prefers. This need, created by a held belief, to get away to find 'IT' only reinforces the illusion that you are separate from God. Enlightenment is never any farther than your own heart and mind.

Everything you need for the journey is already within the space of our own skin. You are equipped with amazing tools in the form of your mind, thoughts and beliefs. Learning to wield these tools consciously and effectively is the beginning of the journey.

- Meditation is the key.
- Understanding how you create with your Beliefs is the door.
- Awareness and conscious living is what you find when you cross the threshold.

Finally, you can think until your head hurts but without action you are passive in the process. Passivity is just another way of not fully, consciously engaging in the process. Reinvigorating or starting a meditation practice is ACTION. Exploring conceptually in your daily life how your thoughts are creative is ACTION. Experimenting and applying new ways of thinking is ACTION. Becoming quiet and exploring your internal landscape is ACTION. Changing a nonproductive thought pattern or a belief that no longer serves you is ACTION. Joining a meditation group is ACTION. Reading an inspiring book is ACTION. Being aware of your breathing is ACTION. Being open to new and different ways of doing things is ACTION.

Chickens, Eggs, Thoughts and Meditation

Which came first, the chicken or the egg? The creative nature of thoughts or meditation? What about Beliefs? Well, they are each distinct yet overlapping. Like an ecosystem they are interdependent on one another. The sum of the parts is greater than the whole. But, being able to disassemble them and look more closely at each will help you understand how they each contribute to this amazing experience called life.

With this in mind, please realize that we are taking a closer look at just a few aspects of your Being—Beliefs and the thoughts that comprise them. Before we get started, I want to be sure that you realize that you are *so much more* than these. Thoughts and Beliefs are building blocks that help to form the foundation for how you create and experience life. But, they are not the only building blocks and tools. While very important to understand and use your Beliefs from a conscious perspective, there is also Fate, Destiny, Co-Creation, Intuition and SO much more at play. I encourage you to explore and engage more consciously with the whole process.

For now, your thoughts create whether you are present or not. Might as well jump in there.

Gravity, Houses and Thoughts

Gravity is a law of the physical world and you have a keen understanding and acceptance of how to move through life using it to your advantage. Doing so certainly makes your life more pleasant if not easier. Regardless of whether you understand the physics of gravity or not, you are still beholden to its influence. Even if you were to dismiss it as so much ridiculousness it would still exist and you would still have to operate within its bounds.

When you drop something, smash your car, spill a cup of coffee or get caught in the rain you don't say that gravity did these things to you. You recognize that you did something that resulted in the smashed car, spilt coffee, etc. Your choices, conscious or not, set the influence of gravity into motion. Actually, its influence is always present, *your choice just made you aware of it*. As with any Law, its influence is pervasive and constant. Like our legal system, ignorance of the Law does not absolve you from the responsibility of adhering to it or the consequences if you don't.

Imagine a beautiful painting, the Mona Lisa. We all know that Leonardo da Vinci painted her. And he operated within the law of gravity to do so. It would be silly to say that gravity painted the Mona Lisa, but it does hold the paint to the canvas. Similarly, an understanding of gravity allowed the great pyramids to be built; allows them to continue to exist by holding them in place.

These are certainly odd examples of the influence of gravity. Not the typical ones that are usually used, like falling apples and breaking glass. My reason for choosing these is to demonstrate that gravity impacts every aspect of your life. I want you to think outside the box and recognize that where there is a Law there is pervasive influence.

Imagine what your life would be like if you periodically decided to be unaware of gravity? Ignore it? WOW! Besides the obvious results, would that mean that it stops existing? That it would no longer exert its influence on you? Of course not. The same is true regarding the LAW that your thoughts are creative. It is not a question of IF but of HOW. You are creating with your thoughts whether you chose to be aware of this or not. And like gravity, this process by which thoughts create is not ego invested in what you do. It is simply a LAW that you operate within and through. Understanding how you are currently doing this and how to do it more consciously is the key.

When you build a house, the first thing you do is lay the foundation. Imagine the whole crew is there; the person that creates the frame for the foundation, the architect, the cement truck driver, the person with the giant squeegee thing to smooth the concrete and everyone else that is needed. The only instructions given are to build a foundation and everyone jumps in at the same time. The odds of creating a functional foundation for your home are not good. You may end up with one that seems to function but then some event occurs— flood, earthquake, hurricane or ground settling—and the true usefulness of your new foundation becomes evident.

The foundation for your experience of life is laid with your thoughts and beliefs. The more conscious you are of how you lay this foundation and the more consistent and consciously engaged you are in that process will determine the quality of your foundation.

In a nutshell, your thoughts create in three distinct yet overlapping ways.

1. Thoughts create matter. Every human made thing was at first a thought in someone's mind. EVERYTHING.
2. Thoughts attract circumstances, people and states of being into your life that have similar qualities as those same thoughts.
3. Thoughts form beliefs, which determine how you experience everything. What you believe about something is how you experience it.

There will be more about all three, especially Beliefs, later. For now, know that they are the stuff that your foundation is made of. Your level of consistent conscious engagement with them is the quality component. If you pay little or no attention to your thoughts and what you are creating with them it is very easy to conclude what sort of foundation you will have for life; unstable, weak, disjointed. However, if you explore the creative nature of thoughts, how you are creating with them and learn how to change Beliefs when they do not serve you, you will create a firm and useful foundation.

For Notes, Thoughts and Ponderings

The Big Three
Matter, Attraction and Beliefs

You have thoughts about everything and everyone that you encounter. You have thoughts about things that you read about, see on TV or the Internet and hear about from other people. You have thoughts about things you imagine might happen and certainly about things that have already happened. All of these thoughts come together to form the foundation for how you experience your past, present and future life.

You are a thought-producing machine; constantly producing and releasing energy in the form of your thoughts. There is never a time when you are not thinking. Thoughts take the form of inner dialogue, images and even sound. From memories to ideas about the future, to what to buy at the grocery store, your brain and mind are doing in tandem what they were designed to do —think—and by their nature they are perfect at this.

All of this thinking is energy and it has to go somewhere. It has to do something. Your head hasn't exploded. Well not literally, so what is happening to this energy? From a physiological perspective, thoughts are a series of chemical reactions in the brain: the release and transformation of energy. From a metaphysical perspective this energy is creating or will create when combined with action and other thoughts. So how and what is all of that thought-energy creating?

Take a look around you right now. *Every man-made thing was first a thought in someone's mind.* EVERYTHING. Don't pass over this amazing truth. Set the book down and take a real good look. If you are inside, look at the paint, light fixtures, furniture, art work, this book, your clothing. Absolutely EVERYTHING. Even you! **This is the first way thoughts create. They create matter.**

All things begin as thoughts. As we lay the foundation for this book and our lives, this incredible Truth is essential to acknowledge, understand and accept. From the very simple to the complex, thoughts are becoming matter all around and through each of us. The only variables are how many thoughts are needed and how much time it takes to manifest them.

Scribbling a note or sending an email takes far less thought and energy to manifest than creating a piece of hand carved furniture or designing a website. However, each must begin with a thought. The more conscious and consistent the thoughts, the greater likelihood that you get the result you desire when you combine them with action.

Consider something you have created. It could be tangible like a painting, a piece of jewelry or a letter to a friend. Or maybe something less tangible like planning and throwing a party, picking up litter at the beach or volunteering. Each of these was preceded by many thoughts. It seems obvious to say so but much of the time, and necessarily so, you don't have to consciously consider the creative thought process; the mechanics of it. You don't say to yourself, *"I am now going to create with my thoughts."* You'd drive yourself crazy if you did. But for the sake of understanding more intimately how the process works, I want you to do just that. It is important that you become aware of how much you think. Important because all of that thinking is creating.

A fun and eye-opening way to begin to consciously acknowledge the creative nature of your thoughts is to spend some time each day noticing the results of your thoughts.

When you wake up tomorrow morning, before your feet even hit the floor, notice your thoughts. If your mind was not thinking you would not even get out of bed. Coffee? Your bladder? Both? The day ahead? Feed the furry friends? Even on those mornings when you feel as if you are sleep walking you ARE thinking.

Let's say that one of the first things you do after getting out of bed is make coffee. Talk yourself through that process. Notice all of the thoughts that need to happen in order for you to make coffee. Even though you do it every morning, thoughts are still needed to get the java going. It's kind of like breathing. Even though you're not conscious of every breath, you are still breathing. It is the same with thinking.

Now, back to the coffee. Maybe your thought process is similar to this:

The coffee is in the kitchen. I have to get out of bed in order to make it. Rinse yesterday's residue out of the pot. Refill the pot. The canister is on the counter. Scoop out enough for 2 cups. Pour the water in the maker. Put the basket in the maker. Push the button.'

Maybe your routine is to stop and get a cup of coffee on your way to work. In that case you have quite a few more thoughts involved—driving, location, etc. Silly as it may seem, walk and talk yourself through this tomorrow morning. The purpose is help you realize how even simple things require a lot of thought. When you pay close, conscious attention to even a simple, mundane task you also pop into the Now. More about this later.

The second way that thoughts create is through attraction. They not only attract circumstances and people to you but, propel you towards the same. So what does that mean? Support groups, fan clubs, friends with similar interests and outlooks are all the result of *thoughts attracting circumstances and people into your life.* Meeting that person who shares our same sense of humor, stumbling across the perfect book and finding the inspiration to change your life. The same occurs with fear-based thoughts too. Fearful thoughts about crime, money, health and all sorts of things can attract those very things and experiences into your life.

Attraction is also at work when you think, *"I need groceries."* While you don't produce the food or grow the vegetables, your thought still begins the process of attracting/creating (bringing into your life) groceries. If you did not think about the need for groceries you would never get them. Gas in your car? You have to think about needing gas before you end up at the gas station filling your car up. Like the earlier gravity examples, these are unusual examples with the purpose of helping you to realize how pervasively your thoughts attract into your life.

On to Beliefs now, but we will come back to this later. I just want to lay the 'foundation' of how your thoughts create and get you THINKING.

The third way that your thoughts create is through beliefs. When you string together enough thoughts and conclusions about a certain thing, person, subject or experience, a belief is created. You have beliefs about EVERYTHING; from why you mow the lawn, or not, to whether God exists and everything in between. Beliefs are what you use to define both your internal and external world and the experience of both. You cannot have an experience without a belief preceding the experience. STOP and consider the importance of this Truth:

Every experience is preceded by a belief. You only experience things— circumstances, people, etc.—that you have thoughts or beliefs about.

This is another one of those Truths that is so obvious that you may tend to look right through it. If you really don't care (have a belief) about something then you don't have an experience of it.

Picture (using thoughts) you and a friend sitting on a park bench and 'something' happens in front of the two of you. When the 'something' is finished happening your friend says, "WOW! That was amazing! I feel as if my life has been changed forever in such a positive way." You react with, "That was so disturbing! I hope that I never experience that again." The thing that happened was neutral. It was not inherently positive or negative. What creates these two very different experiences? Your differing beliefs *about* what happened. Differing beliefs is why there are so many passions and experiences around everyday occurrences; politics, religion, spirituality, sex, education, morality, ethics, philosophy and so on. You don't experience anything until you first decide what it means to you.

Beliefs are subjective and relative. And yet, people state them and approach them as if they are immutable, constant and, well, truth. Nothing could be farther from the TRUTH. That's not to say that holding certain beliefs is not useful or wise. The belief that you should stop at red lights is a good one to have. BUT, it is still a choice to believe that. What makes it an easy choice to make is that you know the consequences of not believing that it is good to stop at red lights. With many, if not most beliefs, you are on autopilot and don't consciously know what or why you believe what you do, let alone the consequences. (more on this later, much more)

It takes a lot of energy and action to create in the physical world. In your non-physical world, no action is required to create other than your thoughts. The quality and characteristics of your thoughts create your internal landscape and your general outlook on life, your experience of life.

Building on the house analogy, the general tone and quality of your thoughts is how you furnish your home. When your thoughts are negative and pessimistic you attract people and circumstances that mirror this view. If you think outside of the proverbial box and approach problems as riddles to be solved and are open to new solutions then chances are you have a life that mirrors that. If your thinking and beliefs are rigid and closed, you probably tend to have a life experience that is limited and closed to opportunities no matter what they may be.

Most of you will usually say that you are generally optimistic and positive. The proof is in the pudding though.

How is your life decorated? Are the people, including family, positive and supportive? Is there always a bit of drama going on? Are YOU dramatic? Self centered?

You can easily see where your thoughts are on the quality scale by what is generally happening in your life and how you handle it. Everyone's life has a great many experiences and events. I don't know of anyone who has a fairytale life. But, overall, what is the tone of your day to day experience of life? The quality of your life? I'm not talking about material stuff or money. Are you content most of the time? Happy? Sad? Angry? Unsettled? Joyful? Are you even able to determine what the general tone of your life is? Are there too many to choose from?

(**Caveat:** I know that life is not always a Pollyanna experience. Many things that we experience are less than pleasant, positive and uplifting—at the time. Having a wide range of emotional experiences and responses is healthy and normal. Grief, sadness, happiness, joy and contentment are all part of life. However, manufacturing a constant string of these states of being based solely on things that occurred in the past or might occur in the future is not healthy or spiritually enhancing.)

How do you FEEL when you think the statement " Life sucks?" or "This always happens to me?" or when you gossip about someone? Negative thinking creates negative perspectives and experiences. It's as simple as that. Change a thought and change how you feel. Change many thoughts and you will change how you feel a lot of the time. This is one of those Truths that has become clichéd with its mainstream acceptance.

I imagine that some of you, when reading the past several paragraphs, zoned out and said to yourself, "Well, of course that's true, duh?" or just skipped ahead. STOP! Remember how I said that Truths and the principles that underpin them, are simple? This is one of those Truths---negative thinking creates negative feelings and perspectives. I could make it more convoluted and complicated for you but why?

Pessimistic, negative, critical thinking creates feelings and states of being that are less than positive and uplifting. String enough of them together and your whole day is crappy. String enough crappy days together and your week sucks. Enough weeks and.....you get the picture. Easy to see in other people, but more important to notice when you are doing it. How many times have you told someone something like "You are being negative or should focus more on the positive."? How many instances could the same advice have applied to you?

So, you create this amazing thing you call your life with the first two ways that thoughts create—**MATTER** and **ATTRACTION**. Then you define and experience life through your **BELIEFS**. How amazing is that?! How powerful is that?

For Notes, Thoughts and Ponderings

What's Getting in the way?

OK, so your thoughts create in three distinct yet overlapping ways—Matter, Attraction and Beliefs. If it is that simple then why aren't you consciously engaged in the process? Why aren't you able to see your role in the creative process? As I mentioned earlier, you are on autopilot most of the time. You do not pay attention to what you think, let alone the qualities and characteristics of those thoughts or their results. Oh sure, when you bump up against results that you don't like or that you aren't sure how to handle you suddenly become conscious. Ah ha, but you are then *only conscious of the results of your thoughts not the thoughts that created the consequences.*

Much of the time you forget that life is happening with a great deal of input from YOU. You may concede that the good and neutral stuff might be a result of your choices and actions. But, the negative or undesirable stuff is certainly 'not yours'. The reason for this is that you fail to see the connection between what you think and what those thoughts create in terms of Matter, Attraction and Belief.

Pretend that you really are the center of the Universe and that there is a laser beam extending out from you registering everything—people, places, circumstances—that occur in and around your life. Slowly turning 360 degrees the radar gathers information and sends it back to you. You then interpret the information and make conclusions about what is going on. Based on these you respond with some combination of actions, words and emotions. You experience.

This is something that you do with your senses, brain and thoughts every day. A lot of the processing, concluding and responding occurs very quickly. Many times you are unaware that this trio has even taken place other than the response or experience part. You simply notice you are experiencing an emotion, your body is in action or something about your state has changed.

Again, *if you are experiencing something or someone then you have had a series of thoughts/ beliefs beforehand.* They may have happened so quickly that you did not notice them, but they happened. Let's say someone cuts you off in traffic. You are *'instantly'* angry, frustrated, scared and boiling. Instantly? Really? Let's slow things down a bit and look closer at what happened before you became that angry, finger waving, tailgating person.

I call this **Stretching The Experience Out.**

You may have thought one or more of the following or something similar and *believed* that the best response and experience was anger, fear, frustration, etc.

- The person is stupid
- The person is careless
- The person was not looking
- The person did it on purpose
- The person shouldn't be driving
- People do this to me all the time
- People cannot drive
- I could have been hurt or killed
- What a jerk

These are Beliefs. And they created your experience of the **neutral** circumstance of being cut off in traffic. WOW! That is quite a series of conclusions and beliefs that fired off in that instant! Look at the list. Of course you experienced anger, fear, frustration, etc. The beliefs that preceded it would not have created a happy experience or even a neutral one. And this all happened in an instant.

Unconscious, fast thinking and concluding is helpful when you stumble and need to steady and prevent yourself from falling. You would land flat on our face if you had to consciously move through that process. But, are all of the beliefs in this example of benefit to you?

When you find yourself only aware of the end result - whether that result is frustration, anger and resentment or joy, elation and contentment - that is the time to slow it down, stretch it out and see what Beliefs are powering your experiences. Even after doing so you may decide that the response and experience that you had was the most beneficial for you at that moment. I would hazard a guess that, upon closer inspection, you will discover that some of your beliefs don't actually serve you in a positive way and that coming to a new belief is in your best interest.

In the traffic example, there is only one Belief that is helpful. Do you know which one that is? And Why?

I could have been hurt or killed

This Belief provides the awareness and needed energy to respond to the situation in a way that truly could benefit you. The rest of the beliefs just create emotional and experience chatter.

For life's more challenging and complicated events, slowing down and moving consciously through the process is essential in order to grow and evolve in a healthy and spiritually aware way.

Emotions

The emotions created by your beliefs are complex, powerful experiences and motivators; sadness, joy, envy, happiness, surprise, anger, love, etc. If you believe that something is fun, exciting or pleasurable then you have an emotional experience of say joy or happiness. If you believe that the same thing is sad, unpleasant and disturbing then you have an emotional experience that is sad or depressing. Again, what you believe creates your experience.

Consider death. Yeah, I know heavy, but stick with me. I am using death because each one of us has very strong beliefs about it resulting in very pronounced emotions being created. Just the mention of death generates an experience in the same instant manner as the getting cut off in traffic example. If you can dissect the conclusions and beliefs that you hold about this major life event then you can surely recognize the more routine patterns that drive your daily experiences. For now, just consider the questions below and you will realize how relative experience is to what you believe.

- Is Death a sad experience?
- Death of a loved one?
- Death of a tyrant?
- How about an elderly person's death versus a child?
- A terminally ill person?
- A healthy person?
- A victim of crime? Murder?
- Death of a stranger?

Death is not inherently sad or any other particular quality of experience. You have general beliefs about Death and specific beliefs about certain deaths, and then you experience them. Knowing what beliefs precede your experience of a particular death may not change the experience, but it does enable you to consciously choose, create and understand this major life experience.

Hindsight

Every experience is relative; is determined by perspective. Expressions like *'Hindsight is 20/20'* and *'Time heals all wounds'* state an essential Truth about the creative nature of beliefs. With the passage of time, your perspectives sometimes change, resulting in your beliefs changing and creating a different experience of the same event.

We have all had experiences of people, places and circumstances that, at the time, seem insurmountable or at the least annoying. Perhaps the experience is joyous and positive. But, after the passage of time we come to view and then BELIEVE differently about what happened. The original event does not change but our experience of it has.

This happens with many experiences and circumstances. Loss of a job, gaining of a job, relationships of all types, rude encounters, pleasant encounters. That is amazing! While you can't rewrite history *you can rewrite your experience of it* and its impact, by changing your Beliefs.

Now, before you start concluding that any 'negative' thoughts are negative, what about thoughts that result in say Fear? Or Anger? Neither is necessarily a bad or negative experience. Neither are fear and anger always the result of less-aware thinking.

Here is an example; you are on a hike when there is a rustle up a head in the bushes and a rattling noise. Was that a rattlesnake? Then just a few feet ahead you see the rattler slithering across your intended path. A certain amount of Fear, based on what you know and believe about rattlesnakes is natural and helpful. Fear can make you cautious when you need to be and give you the energy to heighten you senses and physical abilities. Change the setting to an urban one and imagine that someone is following you to your car in a garage. Maybe you are at the beach and it begins to cloud and thunder. A 'healthy fear' of lightening is a good fear to have.

What about fear of the future, death, crime, nuclear war, economic collapse and others? Fear of simple, everyday things that are only in your mind, which may or may not happen - social situations, losing a job, speaking in front of people, fear of abandonment or being alone? If some of these things DID happen they would be major life events. Anything is possible. Is it probable or only possible that these things will happen? How much of the probability is manufactured in your mind?

As Neale Donald Walsch, author of *Conversations With God*, states in his material, *'Caution is not the same as fear.'* It is good to be cautious in any number of situations. But are you fearful and cautious in situations that don't merit that response? Do you run around feeling afraid of spiders even when you don't see them?

Don't get stuck and pound on yourself because you have a less than 'sunshiny' thought or experience. Rather, determine if the belief and experience is useful. As I mentioned earlier, some negative beliefs and experiences later come to seem very positive and desirable once their full effect is realized with the passage of time. I can't recall where I heard it or whom it is attributed to but *'If you can't do anything about it, why worry? If you can do something about it, why worry?'*

Ronald Lawrence Hays

For Notes, Thoughts and Ponderings

Labeling

Labeling is a short-cut version of thinking, concluding and believing. The following are some of the words used to label situations, circumstances, experiences, beliefs and people:

- negative
- positive
- good
- bad
- ridiculous
- spiritual
- non-spiritual
- right
- wrong

Each label comes with its own thoughts, conclusions and beliefs hidden beneath the tip of the iceberg. When you say, "That's wrong!" all of the thoughts, evidence and beliefs that are necessary when encountering something that is 'wrong' fall into place and you move right into the experience. You skip right past exploring, analyzing and considering and go directly to conclusion and judgment.

Labeling People

Sometimes, labeling can serve you well and is perfectly OK. Like the tripping example from earlier, you would drive yourself crazy if you had to be aware of every thought required in that situation. But, have you ever formed an opinion about someone based solely on a first impression or second-hand information? Maybe you decided they were aloof. So, you interact with them as if they ARE aloof. Aloof is your label and everything that goes along with how you interact and feel about aloof people kicks in with this person. Then you have the opportunity to have lunch with this person and discover that they ARE NOT aloof. Gotta change your label; maybe to friendly or interesting or kind.

Labeling Situations

You do this labeling with situations too. "This is going to be such fun!" Having labeled a situation as fun created an expectation, a pre-experience if you will. When you get there and it really isn't that much fun you change your label to 'boring' or 'not so much fun'. The opposite can happen too. When you are fearful and apprehensive about something, expect it to be unpleasant, you may label it scary, ridiculous or uninteresting. If you go through with it anyway and it is turns out to be different than you labeled it.......you get the picture.

It is a good idea to recognize when you are labeling and spend a few minutes determining if you have the best, most accurate label. Is it based on past experience? Someone else's experience or input? On unfounded fear? It is also beneficial to understand what you put into motion when you do apply a label. If you say something is Good or Bad, what does that mean? What if you label something Negative or Wrong!? What about labeling something Blasphemous or Stupid? Remember the getting cut off in traffic example? Similarly, much comes into play when you use labels.

For Notes, Thoughts and Ponderings

Chatter, Chatter, Chatter

Beliefs, labels, thoughts, creating, attracting, energy!! Your brain and mind are thinking machines, which can produce a lot of chatter. For the sake of *You Believe, You Experience,* Chatter is the kind of thinking that just seems to rattle on with a "mind" of its own. I am talking about the endless processing, analyzing, criticizing and rationalizing. Then there is the perpetual obsessive, compulsive, incessant inner dialogue; jumping to the past and then catapulting to the future. Thinking that is laced with fear and frustration, regret and disillusionment. Your mind creates all sorts of scenarios, the impact of which is stress, anxiety, general fear and discontent.

What if? If I had only? Suppose? Should?

Chatter is the kind of thinking that goes around in circles. It creates that anxious feeling in your chest. There is nothing clear about chatter except that it spirals out of control with one fear or assumption building on another. It can also be on the other end of the spectrum focusing on unrealistic, manic expectations that appear positive on the surface but are actually creating a view of your life that is not realistic or accurate; pie in the sky schemes or convincing yourself that you have won the lottery when you haven't even purchased a ticket.

When Chatter is present, there is no room for lasting contentment or peace. Chatter can revolve around any aspect of life—health, money, God, relationships, death, career, gosh even the traffic you encounter on the way to work or the line at the grocery store. It is easiest to recognize and relate to when it has to do with the BIG areas---money, relationships, health---but it happens with the small stuff too.

Here's how Chatter sometimes happens with money. " I don't have enough money for my rent. What am I gonna do? I can't bring myself to ask someone to loan me money. I am going to be evicted. Well maybe I can pay a few days late. I never have enough money! Why bother even trying to make all of my bills? Just forget it, I can't even find a part-time job in this economy. Besides, even if I did find a part-time job it wouldn't be enough to really help. I am so scared. I am going to lose my apartment, my home, my car. I'll be eating at the Salvation Army! OK, stop it! I am being silly. I am just a little short on the mortgage. I can take that from this other bill. Oh, then I will be late on that one. What about my credit rating if I do that?" And so on.

Relationships and Chatter, now that's one we can all relate to. "Do they like me?, Why don't they like me?, They don't like me., Is this the one?, Oh never mind I'm not gonna be the one to get dumped., Are they cheating on me?, I am just not attractive enough. You get the picture?

Using the examples of money and relationships may seem a bit trite. However, I chose them because most of us can relate to them. To get an even wider view of when and how Chatter happens for you, just substitute anything else in your life in these examples and see how the chatter statements still work or would be similar. Woulda, shoulda, coulda.

(Yes, more on this later—how to identify and stop chatter. Remember, right now we are laying the foundation for understanding how we think and how thoughts create)

Ronald Lawrence Hays

Why all this Chatter?

Why all this Chatter? It has to do with the fact that while you are busy 'doing' things all of time, you are rarely engaged in anything. Running here, going there, buying this, shopping for that, cleaning this, exercising, eating, seeing this movie, watching that show, reading this book, intellectualizing this, etc. Essentially, constantly doing rather than being. Ok, I know, what kind of New Age pabulum is that?

Let me see if I can sort that out. All of this doing is usually based on what you THINK (or others think) you should be doing, *rather than what you BELIEVE and FEEL you would like to do.* You follow your mind rather than your heart or gut. You know what I mean ☺ You have each felt that ping in your heart and that sickening feeling in your gut when you don't follow your instinct. Could be something simple like what clothes to wear or what to have for lunch. Or it could be something major, like who to date or where to live.

Why don't you hear that voice on a daily basis? Usually because your mind is running the show---chattering. Just as often, you let outside influences—TV, media, Internet, family, strangers—determine what you think, believe and DO. You accept the beliefs of others rather than forming your own. Being aware of the beliefs and perspectives of others does not mean you have to adopt them as your own.

How much of the information that you get from sources outside of your own direct experience is of true value to you? Do you really have to form an opinion and then experience everything you are exposed to? While being informed of what is happening in your community and the world at large is a necessity, you do not have to have a passionate response to everything that comes along.

Materials, Tools and a Mess

Imagine going to a home improvement store and buying a saw, a bag of nails, some 2X4s and plywood to make a workbench or a bookshelf. You get home, throw the boards and plywood in the middle of your work area, empty the nails onto the pile of wood, plug-in the saw, turn it on and toss it on top of the pile. It becomes an unusable heap of useful things. That's pretty much what you do with the creative nature of your thoughts everyday. You do not utilize these amazing tools and consciously engage with the process—thus creating chatter.

Jobs, relationships, income and health can all be affected. Sometimes you are able to stay focused in one area, say your career, but the other areas falter. Or you have great relationships with family and friends but can never manage to pay your rent or deal with health issues when they arise.

Chatter also gets in the way of you being able to hear and stick with the guidance of your intuitive, inner voice. You may get an intuitive, beneath the chatter "hit" to pursue something in particular. Initially you'll start out the gate running but the chatter soon drowns out that inner voice causing you to be distracted from its guidance, thus, causing you to loose sight of what you were pursuing and why. You forget how sure you were of the direction to begin with, you abandon it and head off somewhere else; rarely bringing to fruition the things that your inner voice tells you to pursue. This isn't just about things in the physical world. Personal growth and spiritual awareness goals suffer as well.

Your 'hit' might be something simple like 'get off the couch', 'stop being negative' or 'eat better'. Chatter prevents you from hearing these clearly and taking action. Being in the chatter makes it impossible to focus and deal with not only small things that happen in life but major life events too. Moving, death, buying a house, changing jobs, starting new relationships, ending relationships, health issues, etc.; all of these require the ability to focus and fully explore, experience and process them in order to transcend them and ultimately grow. Chatter does not allow this to happen. Thus, your emotional, mental and spiritual well-being is left 'half done'.

Finally, Chatter prevents deep exploration of life's most important and challenging questions and wonderings. What is the purpose of life? Does God exist? Why am I here?

For Notes, Thoughts and Ponderings

Quieting the Chatter

I am not beating up on any of you. I am just pointing out how you create the Chatter. You can only change what you understand and acknowledge what needs changing. You are designed to think, so if you don't get in there and direct the process then it is similar to tossing that saw onto the pile; it creates a bunch of noise and accomplishes nothing that you set out to accomplish.

The result of all of this Chatter is that both WHAT you create and HOW you experience life is inconsistent. You are at the whim of whatever comes along. You might consciously engage for a period of time, see results and then let the chatter take over, failing to recognize that you are lost again. You start something and don't finish. You pursue a goal or a dream and then stop before it comes to fruition.

When you are in the Chatter, your internal landscape— feelings, emotions and your general state of being—is more apt to feel stressed and experience extremes in mood. The longer you stay in the chatter, the more generally discontent you will become and remain.

If you had a scale with which to measure out and weigh your thoughts - on one side would be thoughts that are generally on the productive, positive and constructive nature; on the other side, thoughts that are negative, worrisome and generally destructive in nature (chatter). In what direction would your scale tip? Not sure? Consider, how do you generally feel in your daily life? That feeling is the cumulative effect, the overall quality, of your thoughts on a daily, weekly, yearly basis.

Please don't conclude that if you understand the creative nature of thoughts, develop a meditation practice and learn how to get beneath the Chatter that life will always be a bowl of cherries; that Snow White will be in your kitchen everyday making your coffee and singing with Bluebirds. LIFE is full of endless possibilities and experiences and not all of them are what we might want—at the moment. In other words, some of it sucks—even if you do explore the creative nature of your thoughts, meditate and manage to get beneath the Chatter every day.

Which brings me back to something that I said earlier. You are more than your thoughts. This is the perfect spot to pause and consider that you are only looking at one aspect of the creative process and yourself: the creative nature of your thoughts, how they create, form beliefs and create your experiences and how to become more consciously engaged in that process. But, let's not forget that co-creation is at work. Toss in Fate and Destiny and a blend of collective consciousness too! We are looking at the building blocks, the glue, the basics, the tools.

The reason I stress this again now is because it is a TRUTH. Your mind, thoughts, and consciousness are tools to be wielded:

- To explore the meaning of your existence and life.
- To be applied to enhance your life;
- Harnessed to make the journey through Fate, Destiny, co-creation and collective consciousness.
- To define who you are in relationship to all of the above.

As you move into the next part of your journey, keep this question in mind, *"How can I use these tools to explore the many aspects of my being and existence?"*

Getting Beneath The Chatter

Quieting your mind is what I call *getting beneath the chatter*. **Getting beneath the Chatter allows you to respond rather than react.** It helps you to see where you might have played a part in what has happened. It helps you to decide how you will experience and finally what that experience will mean for you. The more you are able to quiet your mind, the more aware you become and the more you get to define who you are with conscious, directed choices and beliefs—not chatter.

Getting beneath the Chatter does not necessarily mean entering a place that is constantly void of all thoughts, images and dialogue. Think of it as being beneath the surface of the ocean or a lake. Despite what is happening above the water, you enter a whole other world. While you are below exploring, life above continues with all of its own beauty. There may even be a storm above and you are nestled below while anyone on the surface is being tossed about and battered by winds and rain.

So it is with getting beneath the Chatter. You simply move into another aspect of awareness that at times may be very quiet and calm and at others can be teaming with activity in the form of thoughts, images and inner dialogue. You may not always get to choose which it is, but you will always benefit from being there.

To a certain extent, we each move in and out of the Chatter. It is part of the rhythm of awareness. A certain amount of Chatter allows you to make it through some pretty mundane tasks that you don't need to be consciously thinking about every step of the way. The bottom line is—you are human. Like everything else in the Universe you are moving and changing and do not remain in any one state constantly. You certainly do not stay beneath the Chatter 24/7. You are a spiritual being having a human experience and therefore you will move in and out of SPIRITUAL awareness. Just think of those non-aware times as experience gathering; then back to SPIRIT to make a deposit in your awareness account.

It's all fine and dandy to consider how thoughts create and to recognize how chatter interferes with your being able to consciously engage in that process. But, how do you put this understanding to practical use in your life? What do you do when you just can't get out of the noise?

Answer: You develop a regular meditation practice. This is a simple yet not quick or easy thing to accomplish.

Developing a meditation practice is similar to beginning a physical exercise regimen such as weight lifting or jogging or changing your eating habits. It is a lot of work. Remember the last time you started back at the gym? How sore your muscles were? How everyday for the first few weeks you just thought you couldn't take it anymore? Or when you started jogging to lose those few extra pounds? Jog a mile? Yeah right! How about pass out after 1/8th of a mile? With commitment, determination and patience you build up stamina. You don't start out running a marathon.

A sound meditation practice and the benefits that come with it require the same commitment, determination and patience. It also comes with the same pitfalls as physical exercise—fatigue, loss of interest and just plain running out of steam before you begin to see the consistent benefits that you are looking for. If you do stop when you begin to see those benefits then the benefits stop too. Stick with it and meditation will transform your life in much the same way that a regular physical exercise regimen will transform your body and health.

By telling your mind what to focus or concentrate on, a meditation practice enables you to get beneath the chatter *at will* and for extended periods of time. You get to take charge. Each of you is already doing this; you just don't recognize it as meditation because of preconceived ideas and beliefs that you may hold about meditation.

Just as your thoughts create in three distinct yet overlapping ways, a meditation practice accomplishes in three distinct yet overlapping ways:

- It quiets your mind
- Brings you into the NOW
- Shifts your perspective`

The result of all three is that you become more consciously engaged in life's creative process.

In addition to all of the exercises and tools to come, here are a few general suggestions for how to best get a good solid, manageable start with your meditation practice or jumpstarting one that has fallen by the wayside:

- Remember that it is simple, not easy

- Practice daily

- Turn off your TV for the first 30 days

- Limit your computer time to just the necessary things.

- Be conscious of your breathing throughout the day

- Join a meditation group or find a friend who would like to meditate together once a week

- View this as fun and exciting (because it is)

Meditation, What is it?

What is Meditation? There are a lot of ideas, definitions, techniques and beliefs surrounding meditation-so where to start? Which one to choose? Do any of them really have the answers? Yes. Each of you knows the answer for you. You just have to find it.

Meditation is a word that comes with a lot of preconceived ideas. Many of these ideas have their roots in Eastern religion and philosophy. Words like Guru and Buddhist come to mind. Meditation may conjure visions of sitting cross-legged on the floor with your hands turned upward. Long robes and beaded hair, sandals, vegetarianism and vows of silence. Some people would say that is because meditation is Eastern or at least is rooted there.

While some meditation techniques and schools of thought may be Eastern, meditation itself is Universal. Meditation is only a term for the practice of quieting the mind; a journey within; a conscious connecting with the life force. Every culture has some form of this quieting of the mind in its make-up. Prayer, meditation, solitude, chants, drumming. Don't get hung up on the technique or the term. Get hung up on the doing and the being—get hung up on the experience and result of meditation.

If you research definitions of the word meditation you will see certain words or phrases come up time and again. The common denominators are: a practice, regular, spiritual/religious, and regimen. When you start to define types of meditation then terms like Eastern, Western, Tibetan and others come into play. What do all of these regular spiritual/religious practices or regimens accomplish regardless of the origin of their technique? They help to relax and quite your mind and bring you to the Now.

There are no grounds more foreign to your spirit than the past and the future. Your mind on the other hand is more comfortable in either of these places than in The Now. If you are in the past or the future your mind is running the show. Unless you consciously go to the past to retrieve and learn or go to the future to create. What's the difference? Coming to the NOW with meditation and then sending your mind in either direction.

When people mountain climb or repel, they anchor their safety cable, ensure that their harness is secure and then lower themselves down the mountain face or climb upwards. Slowly and deliberately they go in either direction, all the while firmly anchored. They explore and eventually return to where they are anchored. They would never begin a climb without being assured that all of the appropriate safety precautions are in place. The same should be true of your trips to the past or future. Be sure that you are firmly anchored in the now. Meditation will help you do that.

Children thrive when there is love, structure and discipline in their world, helping them to grow, evolve and mature. Complete lack of OR overbearing love, structure and discipline can cause children to develop all sorts of emotional, physical and mental issues. It is similar when your mind is allowed to run the show. Meditation is providing the perfect loving, structured and nurturing environment for your mind to enable you to grow and expand in awareness of self and the greater whole.

Simply put, my definition of meditation is,

Giving your mind a task rather than letting it give you the task.

With this definition, meditation and the state that it produces, can take place anytime, anywhere and with any activity. You don't have to be surrounded by silence and incense and sitting cross-legged on the floor. Though that is very conducive, so are many other situations. If you wait for the 'perfect' conditions to meditate--quiet, soft light, wooded location, mountain trail, the beach, workshops, you are missing the point and the benefits. Those settings put you into a meditative state with little or no effort on your part. They help to provide powerful meditative experiences and should certainly be sought out on a regular basis. I encourage you to also seek out less conducive settings with that same fervor. These less conducive settings will open up your whole life to the tremendous benefits of meditation. An important element of a meditation practice is to be able to get into a meditative state even in imperfect settings. Find the calm in the eye of the storm.

- In a crowded room
- On a plane

- At the mall
- With the kids screaming in the background
- A hospital waiting room
- Your desk at work
- Standing in line at the grocery store
- Sitting in the drive thru at the bank
- At the symphony
- Walking down the street

You get the point? *You can meditate ANYWHERE* and the challenges of some places will strengthen your practice. This also allows your practice to be with you wherever you are.

Beliefs that impede meditation

In order to reap the benefits of meditation you have to engage in it on a consistent basis. As mentioned previously, if you believe that you need the perfect circumstances in order to mediate then you may need to change some of your beliefs. Those perfect conditions can be considered classroom time. The less conducive settings can be testing and strengthening time.

The way to change a belief about needing certain conditions for meditation is to first consider the possibility that conditions are not necessary in order to meditate. Then, EXPERIENCE that this is true by meditating in less than conducive settings. Like physical conditioning, this may be difficult at first, but persevere.

Try this exercise: Take 5 minutes, 3 times a day, close your eyes, breathe and go within. Quiet your mind and meditate in different, 'unusual places'. Try the line at the drive-thru teller, the food court at the mall, on a park bench, in your office, while sitting at that 10-minute red light or in a hospital waiting room. Do you have a cell phone or a watch with a timer? Set it for the 5 minutes and drift beneath. Don't have a timer? Go to a dollar store and get one. But don't use lack of a timer as an excuse not to begin this little, manageable exercise TODAY.

The purpose of this exercise is to help you begin to shed your belief that certain conditions are needed in order to meditate and to start bringing meditation out of the 15 minute, twice daily box that you may have it tucked into. At first it may be very challenging. Expect it to be. Your mind may try to convince you to feel silly and self-conscious or just plain ridiculous. The distractions may be too great at times and you might feel as if there is no meditative benefit because you just aren't 'getting there'. Trust me and give it a couple of weeks of 'training', building up your stamina and strength. You will begin to experience how powerful and empowering this simple exercise will be for you. Remember, you promised to try the exercises and I have kept my promise to keep them simple, with this one ☺

No matter the setting, *BREATHING correctly and consciously is essential to any meditation practice.* Breathing correctly is using your diaphragm to pull your breath down into your lungs, filling them fully. Placing a hand on your chest will help you to be aware of where you are breathing. You want to have minimal movement in your chest, having your stomach poke out as your breath makes it deep into your lungs.

Several beneficial things occur when you pay attention to your breathing and use your diaphragm fully:

- You come into the NOW. This happens because ordinarily you do not have to pay attention to every breath you take. Doing so makes you CONSCIOUS.

- Breathing deeply (belly breathing) is known to release some of your bodies endorphins. Some of which are like natural narcotics---helping you to relax.

- You get beneath the chatter and enter a meditative state.

Learning how to let go of beliefs that require certain conditions in order to be able to meditate will help you to let go of other 'belief blocks' on the road to meditation without limits. Some of these 'belief blocks' may be:

- Meditation must be approached from an Eastern perspective
- Your mind should be blank
- Large amounts of time are needed in order to meditate

Meditation is Universal

Meditation is Universal. The belief that meditation is Eastern can be a difficult one to set aside but as we move through this journey together you will begin to see it slip to the side. The key to changing this one is to be open and consider what every meditation practice has in common- a regular spiritual/religious practice or regimen that quiets the mind--and step out there and try different techniques. You are doing that now just by reading this book. With the new, practical definition that you are exploring here –*giving your mind the task rather than letting it give you the task*- you may choose and explore whatever techniques interest you. You can even develop your own technique for giving your mind the task and getting beneath the chatter.

Your mind does not have to be blank

Another limiting belief is that the goal of meditation is to reach a state where your mind is totally blank. That through concentration and breathing all thoughts, images and dialogue will eventually cease. Your mind by its very nature is never 100% blank. Holding a belief that the mind can be blank is setting yourself up for disappointment and 'failure' when it comes to meditation. This is not to say that the activity of your mind cannot be much, much less and even minimal.

Have you ever curled up to read a book and a few hours later you are still fully engrossed? You wonder, "WOW! Where did the past few hours go?" Consider two things - 1) your mind has been very busy and 2) you have been in a meditative state. Your mind has been performing all sorts of tasks—recognizing and processing the words on the pages, comprehending, visualizing the plot, identifying with characters, wondering what is going to happen. Certainly not blank. And yet you entered a meditative state of mind and being.

Why do I say this is meditative? Notice how you feel during and after these hours of reading? You probably have a sense of satisfaction, pleasure and calm. Your perspective is different, has shifted as you 'returned' and your mind has less chatter. You move into the rest of your day or evening feeling less stress. These are hallmarks of a meditative state.

That's what happens when you give your mind the task rather than letting it give you the task. The task can be most anything:

- reading a book
- running
- gardening
- cleaning the house
- singing
- cooking and
- swimming

Creative activities of any kind:
- writing
- drawing
- sewing
- painting

Everyday activities:

- breathing
- contemplating
- doing the laundry
- staring at the ceiling fan
- conversation with a good friend

It is not the activity but how its approached that makes it meditative.

Sometimes while in a meditative state you may experience a lot of thoughts, images, feelings, etc. You might even dip in and out of little quiet patches. Like a rhythm. One day your mediation may be very quiet and nearly blank and the next day you may have a meditation full of activity. Both can be very meditative and beneficial.

If you are having a mediation with a lot of inner dialogue or what seems to be chatter, take note of what the chatter is saying. Perhaps you are being given an awareness or 'working' on something from a deeper place.

You don't need large amounts of time

The belief that meditation requires awakening at 3:00AM to chant and OM to the Universe for 3 hours, afterwards preparing your fully organic breakfast and then you might be ready to join the world (you know what I mean, don't you? ☺) is only one idea of the amount of time that it takes to meditate. If this scenario were the case, I surely would not meditate regularly. This is not to say that 3 hours of meditation and an organic breakfast are not beneficial. How much time is needed to have a beneficial meditation practice is different for each person. Sometimes it changes from day to day. You decide based on the benefits that you derive from your practice. Fifteen minutes can change your life just as 3 hours may do nothing but exhaust you.

Any belief that limits how, when, where and what you do when you meditate has to go. Or at least be set-aside in order for you to benefit fully from the suggestions that will follow. You can pick them back up again when you are done.

For Notes, Thoughts and Ponderings

Meditation 101

Regardless of how you choose to 'do' meditation the result will be the same. You will reach a state of focus and calm resulting in a sense of well-being. Your perspective will shift and problems and concerns seem more manageable. Joys and pleasures are enhanced. This is a state of feeling rather than emotion. It is not a thoughtless, blank state of mind and being. And usually, time tends to become elastic, like in the reading example. An hour may seem like 5 minutes or 5 minutes like an hour. While there are many ways of 'doing' meditation, there is also great value in being able to sit within the space of your own skin, becoming quiet and exploring your internal landscape.

If meditation is *giving your mind a task* then how do you do that? Well, you start by talking to yourself; talking to your mind actually. I know it goes against what all mental healthcare professionals advise. Seriously though, you have to tell your mind what *not* to do and as well as what *to* do. Expect a lot of resistance. Imagine your mind is like a child that has been allowed free reign for a number of years and then, out of the blue, the parents decide to add a few behavioral expectations. That never goes over well. Actually, things usually get worse before they get better.

This does not mean telling your mind that the house is not on fire when indeed the flames are all around you. It is not about denying reality. It is about experiencing reality as it is NOW and choosing how you will experience that reality. You do this the same way you tell your mind to read a book.

You have to realize that you are not your mind or your thoughts. I know, all wonderful in New Age Theory and even easier to just consider while sitting here reading THIS book. But seriously, you are NOT your mind or your thoughts exclusively. Always remember that your mind and thoughts are just one part of the *Whole You*. You are Mind, Body and Spirit.

Let's explore a few more exercises and tools that will help you build your meditation practice. Use these in tandem with one another throughout your day. Some of them are better suited for certain situations than others. I have designed them that way so that you will always have a tool regardless of what is going on around you. That way your meditation can be with you at all times, as it should be.

Exercises

Talking to your Mind

Purpose: To help you recognize that you are more than your mind; to demonstrate that you can control what happens in your mind.

Talking to your mind is one of the most effective tools for helping you to get beneath the chatter and meditate. Notice that I said talking to your mind and not to YOU. This trick instantly makes you aware that you are NOT your mind. If you say to your mind, *"Stop it!"* you have just moved into a state of awareness that there is some other part of you that can tell your mind what to do. I call it your Higher Self. Your Higher Self uses your mind as the tool it is designed to be, to tell your mind what to do.

The next time your mind is chattering away and you want to meditate, try telling your mind *"I am going to meditate"*. This may seem silly at first and you may feel silly doing it. But, trust me on this one...IT WORKS. This is a tool that you can use anywhere. Well, unless you talk out loud and then you may get carted off. Seriously though, try breathing deeply and telling your mind to *"STOP IT!"* *"Please stop chattering."* You can also repeat the directive NO, over and over to 'drown out' the chatter. *"NO, NO, NO, NO, NO, NO, NO."* This breaks the cycle.

If you want to have a sitting meditation but your mind is running 100-mph just say, *"Slow down. Slow down. Gently, slow down. I want to meditate and things need to be a little slower in here for me to do that."* Continue breathing deeply and on each exhale repeat *"Slow down."* In just a few minutes your mind will usually be quieter and you will be able to start meditating. Gently but firmly tell your mind what the task at hand will be---meditating or just becoming quiet. You may even have to say, *"You do what you want but I am going to meditate. Please don't bother me until I am done."*

Talk to your mind on a regular basis just like you would a dear friend or a small child. *"What shall we do today?"* *"How will you consciously engage with the creative nature of thoughts today?"*

"Notice what you're doing with OUR thoughts." "Pay attention!" "You should focus on something else." "How are you feeling---what thoughts or beliefs contributed to that feeling of joy, stress, happiness, contentment or frustration?" This is not all about the 'negative' in your thoughts either. **It is just as valuable to become aware of how you create positive experiences and states of being.**

10 minutes, eyes closed, breathing. Twice daily.
Purpose: To get you comfortable and familiar with sitting quietly within the space of your own skin.

You don't start out running a marathon and you don't start out with the ability to sit quietly while attempting to meditate. This short, simple exercise is a good place to begin. It is not always easy but the results are powerful. Start out with the commitment to do this exercise each morning and evening for 15 days. Sit comfortably, set a timer or alarm clock for 10 minutes, close your eyes and breathe; in through your nose, out through your mouth. Breathe deeply bringing your breath all the way down into your lungs. Place a hand on your chest for the first minute or so to ensure that there is minimal movement in your upper chest and shoulders when you inhale deeply. Your belly should poke out with each deep inhale. Keep your eyes closed no matter how strong the temptation may be to open them.

The timer allows you to immerse yourself without having to be concerned with time. Closing your eyes shuts out the visual world (and its distractions) allowing you to sit with your internal landscape. The value in this is becoming familiar with what is going on inside of you. All this talk of thoughts and creative nature is fine. However, it helps to recognize what you are thinking, what is in your mind; the general climate if you will. This exercise helps you to see the benefits of sitting quietly and observing your thoughts, emotions, feelings and inner dialogue.

15 minutes, eyes closed, breathing. Twice daily.
Purpose: Builds upon the 10-minute exercise, deepening the awareness of what and how you think in general.

This one pushes the envelope by 5 minutes. Make the commitment to do this exercise for 15 days. As the days go by, you will start to get a general idea of what your internal landscape is like. Some days will be easier and more positive than others. Some mornings the 15 minutes will seem like hours. Some evenings you will swear that there IS NO MORE time for the day. What happens over time is you get a kind of 'average'. A general internal weather report. You will begin to notice patterns of thinking, areas of your life that cause you concern and the overall quality and characteristics of your thoughts. Also, you will begin to notice how WHAT you think creates how you feel and experience.

15 minutes breathing, counting backwards. Twice Daily
Purpose: To bring you into the now, get your mind to step aside and enter a more meditative state.

Now we add a twist. In addition to sitting quietly, eyes closed, breathing deeply with minimal movement in your chest, you will count backwards from 300. On your first inhale count "3" and on the exhale "hundred'. Then on the next inhale "2" and on the exhale "99". Then '2", "98". Continuing to count backwards until your timer goes off. Several things are happening with this deceptively simple tool.

- First, closing your eyes enables you to focus inward (which is where you want to go).
- Second, being aware of your breathing always brings you more into the now---the feel and sensation of it filling and exiting your body.
- Third, counting backward in rhythm with your breath gives your mind a task—enabling it to be "kept busy" rather than chattering.

The result of all three components combined is you enter a deeper meditative state.

I Spy

Purpose: To bring your attention into the now. Especially helpful in busy, noisy, distracting environments. When you can't get quiet enough to even think about meditating.

It is just what it sounds like....the game you played as a child. All you have to do is start noticing everything that is within range of your senses. As you notice something say to yourself, "I see the green leaves on the plant in the corner." "I see the cuticle on my index finger." "I hear the air conditioner and the conversations in the room." "I feel the warmth of the sun." Consciously acknowledge everything. Do this until your mind begins to quiet and you feel calm. This one usually takes a few minutes but is very powerful. Once the benefit kicks in you can then start to breathe and move more into a meditative state.

Sticker on 3rd Eye

Purpose: Helps to draw your focus inward.

Your 3rd Eye is located in between and just above your physical eyes. Place a sticker or piece of tape on your 3rd Eye and then close your physical eyes. Breathe slowly and deeply. You will be amazed at how the presence of the sticker draws your focus inward through your 3rd Eye. To notice the difference, you can experiment by removing it for a minute or so and then placing it back on your 3rd Eye. This is a good one to use in conjunction with any of the other exercises.

What to do once you are Beneath The Chatter?

What do you do once you are able to get beneath the Chatter? Anything you wish to do. We'll explore a few suggestions together but let these be only the beginning of your journey.

You can simply ride the wave as surfers say. Go with the flow. Enjoy the mellow. Get quiet and dip beneath the chatter, relishing in the experience of being in a meditative state with a quieter mind, just being and immersing in your internal landscape. The benefits of this are immeasurable.

So much of your life is spent outside of yourself. The result of becoming comfortable with sitting inside is awareness of who you are aside from all of the external stuff. You begin to notice how you think, what you think and start to become more acutely aware of the often indefinable 'larger picture'. The more you ride the wave the more of a sense of awareness develops. Awareness is a knowing, an assuredness. Awareness is when you are riding the wave and you suddenly realize that you are observing it all. Practice riding the wave!

Try this exercise: Set your timer or alarm clock for 20 to 30 minutes. Sit in a comfortable chair that will support both your body and neck if possible. You may recline if you are sure that you will not fall asleep ☺ With your hand on your chest, breathe deeply using your diaphragm to pull your breathe all the way down into your lungs, causing your stomach to poke out a bit. You want to have minimal movement in your chest. Picture your lungs expanding out at the bottom like a bell as your breath fills them. Your hand on your chest helps to make you aware of where you are breathing. Continue breathing deep and slow—in through your nose and out through your mouth.

Rather than trying to block out any distractions such as noises, temperature or light—notice them, listen to them, and feel them. "Label" them as part of your meditation not a distraction. "Part of" creates a much different reaction and experience than "distraction".

As you begin to relax, start counting backwards from 300 on each exhale. Inhale. Exhale (300). Inhale. Exhale (299).

Inhale. Exhale (298), and so on. Notice your thoughts. Images. Dialogue. Just watch it all—like a movie. At the movies, you don't reach out and try to hold onto what is happening on the screen. How silly that would be. Just let your internal movie play. Simple, but not easy to do. As you begin to dip beneath that chatter, at your own pace, feel and recognize your awareness shift to be the observer of all that you are experiencing at this moment.

Ride the wave frequently. Two or three times daily if you can. The more you practice the stronger you become. The more wonderful experiences you will have. Ultimately, the more benefits you will reap from your meditation practice.

Visualization

Once you are accustomed to riding the wave and the enjoyment of that, try this on for size—use visualization to build an internal Town Center. The genesis for this idea comes from the work of Peter McWilliams. He referred to it as a Sanctuary and I encourage you to look at his material for fascinating and practical suggestions. They are marvelous and all of his material is available free online at *http://www.mcwilliams.com/books/books/*. Of course you may always purchase his books at any bookstore and online booksellers.

Visualization is a wonderful meditative tool for exploring more deeply your inner landscape, understanding your beliefs and how they are creating. It is using your thoughts as the tools they are intended to be. It is using your imagination to

IMAGINE things that you would like to create, situations that you want to understand and truths you want to explore. For additional information on how to use visualization within your meditation practice and in life in general I encourage you to spend some time with the works of Shakti Gawain at *http://www.shaktigawain.com/*.

Visualization is both an amazing tool and a fantastic experience. It has many uses and there are as many techniques as you can, well, visualize. For the sake of what we are doing here, I'll keep it to the basics and how they relate to meditation and beliefs. Again, I strongly encourage you to take a look at the two wonderful teachers mentioned to fully explore visualization.

The Town Center is a place where you can go, using visualization, to explore meditation and beliefs. It will have everything that you need to explore ideas, concerns, possibilities, past experiences, dreams and to conquer fears—anything that you choose to do. A perfectly safe place with no crime, lawsuits or park fees and everything is free. It is the heart of a community and reflects everyone who moves in and through it. Your Town Center will be similar.

Read through the suggestions for creating the Town Center first and then create yours, with the not even the sky as a limit. Afterwards, there will be suggestions on how to use it.

Creating a Town Center

Imagine what the perfect Town Center is for you. It can be Mayberry from the Andy Griffith show or it can be Times Square. It can be Mayberry IN Times Square. It can be a small mountain town or a seaside village; a settlement on the moon or an oasis in the desert. There are no limits in your imagination.

Once you imagine your setting, it is time to add buildings. When I say buildings I mean structures of any kind that you can imagine-up. You may want all of your buildings to be of the same architectural style or have each one reflect a very different style. You can have Tepees, igloos, tree houses, skyscrapers, underwater domes or structures suspended in midair. The weather will always be whatever you want it to be so if it is always 78 degrees you may not want or need walls or roofs.

Now, here are a few suggested 'businesses', 'storefronts' and 'civil establishments' that you will want to consider having in your Town Center and why.

A Library

You will need a place to go for information, for research and learning. I use the term Library, but much like "buildings' this is just a starting point. The key is to build a place to house all of the knowledge of the Universe and a way for you to access it. Computers, staff, or a council of elders, a giant crystal ball. Some mechanism for getting information. Or multiple mechanisms.

Drs. Office/Clinic/Medicine Woman

This is a place for healing mind, body and spirit. Eastern, Western, holistic, modern—you name it. Any combination of approaches, techniques, medicines and healthcare professionals that you feel you need. Unlike healthcare in the real world, everything is free and all modalities are compatible and encouraged.

Mercantile/General Store

This is a place to acquire things that you may want, need or are curious about. Maybe you want to buy paints and a canvas to create a masterpiece. Perhaps you are looking for a special stone to help you focus during meditation. You may even get special clothing or shoes for places you will go exploring.

School/University/College/Wisdom Center

This is a place where you go to learn from other students and Masters. The perfect environment to nurture your desire to learn. Classrooms, workshops even one on one instruction with Masters, you name it and the course is on the schedule.

Movie Theater

A place to watch movies, videos, projections from your past, present and future. Could be like The Rose Bowl, in the midst of Stonehenge, at the bottom of the ocean in a dome or at your local Cineplex.

A Park

Indoors, outdoors, a little of both, in the clouds, near the ocean, in the mountains—you imagine it. Maybe a park setting that changes depending on your mood or what you want to do there. I suggest some place that is only nature. Populate it with animals too if you like.

OK, get to work, get beneath the chatter and build!! And you can always come back and change, add or get rid of anything. Just get it built so that you can get to using it.

Using the Town Center

The best way to teach you how to use the Town Center is to give you a specific task to accomplish with it. So, go to your Town Center and while you are there explore and learn and experience meditation.

First, you will need to get beneath the chatter. Use any of the tools and exercises that we have talked about previously or any new ones that you have picked up or read about. I suggest some form of sitting comfortably and breathing deeply, turning your focus within and making any distractions part of the meditation. Remember to label them 'part of'. Try nodding from side to side just slightly as you close your eyes and continue to breathe.

Once you have been able to quiet your mind, envision yourself in your Town Center. A really helpful place to go when you want to learn is your Library. You can instantly transport to there or you can leisurely stroll along the sidewalks, moonwalks or whatever you have created in your Town Center for getting around. Enjoy the sights, sounds and smells as you make your way to the Library.

Once you get there, ask the Librarian to help you find information on how to improve your meditation practice. Or, if you have a giant crystal ball, ask it to reveal the answers to your questions about meditation. Maybe start with, "How do I improve my ability to get my mind quiet?" If your Library is more like a council of Elders, then go before them and ask them the same question. Then listen for the answer, look through the books or watch for the crystal ball to reveal.

Maybe you want to know what beliefs you hold that are blocking you from fully immersing in the meditation practice regularly. You could pull one of the elders aside and ask them to help you. You might choose to go to the University and take a class on beliefs that impede MY meditation practice. It will be tailored specifically to you.

I encourage you to incorporate visualization and your Town Center into you meditation practice. It is great fun and very beneficial. You can bring any and all questions, contemplations and problems to this safe place.

Meditation and visualization are great tools for helping you to recognize, understand and change Beliefs when necessary. Both empower you to live your life consciously and with purpose. They also help you to define yourself consciously. Beliefs are thoughts and they will create whether you consciously engage in the process or not. (I mentioned this earlier but thought this was a good place to be redundant).

Belief Systems

Just as your Thoughts and Meditation Practice create in three distinct yet overlapping ways, so do your Beliefs:

1. They create your perspectives
2. They determine your experiences
3. They define who you are

Beliefs are a series or collection of thoughts that you have about a particular area or circumstance of life. String enough beliefs together and you get Belief Systems. **A Belief System is a set of ideas, assumptions and conclusions.** You have Belief Systems about politics, spirituality, sexuality, morality, education, war, family, money--everything. For every experience you have, there is a belief or Belief System driving the decisions and actions behind it.

Belief Systems are complex and interrelated. Similar to those mosaic pictures that when you get closer are actually made up of thousands of individual pictures; that's what a belief system is like. It looks simple from far away but as you get closer you start to see how many thoughts come together to create it. When you do not recognize, understand and sometimes change them, your life is created from a series of unconscious reactions and reflexes rather than from a place of consciousness.

While Belief Systems can be complicated and interconnected, identifying and understanding them is simple. As with everything we have done thus far, it takes patience, determination and commitment. The key is to start from the result and work your way back. Margaret Mitchell used this approach when writing her Pulitzer winning novel *Gone With The Wind*. She wrote it from the end to the beginning, backwards. Because beliefs are more than the random thought, but complex groups of thoughts, many times you may not even know what beliefs have gotten you to where you are in your life. But, there is no doubt about where you are—good, bad or indifferent.

If you don't like the quality of your life experience, you have the power to change it by changing your Belief Systems. This doesn't mean that you have to toss all of your beliefs out the window and start from scratch. You just have to change the beliefs that are creating the circumstances and experiences that you do not wish to have.

It is important to draw a distinction between the Law of Attraction teachings and what you are exploring here. This is not about creating in the physical world, attracting things to you. While thoughts do that, you are exploring what you believe and how that creates your *experience* of life. Put another way, this is not about stuff; it is about perspective, experience and the non-tangible aspects of your being. There is a lot of information out there about the Law of Attraction and I invite to you explore that as well. But for now, you are looking at your beliefs. You can even look at your beliefs ABOUT The Law of Attraction. See the difference?

Let's go back to the house analogy. Over the course of time, many parts of a home will need to be replaced or repaired. If your kitchen faucet is leaking you don't bulldoze the whole place! You fix the faucet. The kitchen is a belief system and the faucet is the component of the system that does not work or serve you as well as it once did. It is creating the experience that you do not want. Imagine going 5, 10, or even 20 years without making repairs on your home. Sometimes after years of neglect a complete renovation is needed in order to make a home safe, sound and comfortable again.

It is similar with your beliefs. Consider a belief that you have held for 5, 10 or 20 years that seems silly or useless for the person you are today. When you were younger did you believe that 40 or 50 was old? What happened to that belief when you turned 30? 40? If you've held onto that belief as you reached 40 and beyond, your experience is out of synch with what is true. When this belief is out of synch, many people have what we call a midlife crisis.

You can explore the effects of leaving this Belief System in place by examining what it means FOR YOU to believe that you are old. *'40 is old'* is a belief based on a perspective that you formed when you were younger. 40 does seem old when we are 15 or 20! But it doesn't work when you are 40. And what is old? Remember our getting cut off in traffic example? Let's do the same thing here and 'stretch out' the belief that *'40 is Old'* and then your belief about old.

If you believe that you are Old at 40, you may hold some of the beliefs below. In parentheses I have placed just one example of what each belief may create.

- I am in declining health (fear)
- I am close to death (fear)
- I am past my prime (anger)
- The best of my life is behind me (sadness)
- I am no longer attractive (depressed)
- I have traded my youth for wisdom (bitter)
- I should be somewhere in my life by now (ashamed)
- It's time to 'do something' with my life (anxious)

These beliefs come together to form a Belief System regarding what it is to be OLD. What do you suppose your experience will be if you hold several of these beliefs when you reach an age that you consider to be Old?

What if you replace this Belief System with one that says, *Life begins at 40*? What new beliefs might comprise this new System? What experiences will they create? What if you also change your related Belief System about OLD? The result could be similar to this:

Life Begins at 40

- I am so much wiser (confident)
- I am not even at the halfway point (grateful)
- I have hit my stride (accomplished)
- There is even more good ahead (excited)
- I look better-inside and out (happy)
- I have learned from my youth (wise)
- My life may go where I want it to (assured)
- I can do/be something different with my life (determined)

Quite a different experience, yes?

What is a Foundational Belief System?

This brings us to Foundational Belief Systems (FBS) of which there are four.

- God
- Death
- Material Security
- Sexuality

These are the big ones from which all others spring forth. Everyone has these and what comprises them can differ greatly from person to person. At the heart of what you are doing here is identifying your FBS, understanding what experiences they are creating and then changing them when necessary. You will do this in just the same way as I showed you with the 'getting cut off in traffic' example. Then you'll use the house analogy to work on making any repairs that may be needed.

As you go forward, be sure to have the following readily available:

- paper and pen
- a timer
- a comfortable chair or place to sit and
- a package of multicolored highlighters

You'll spend one week with each of the four FBS. By the end of the four weeks you will have a pretty good awareness of each and what types of experiences they create in your life. You will also be able to move on to explore any other belief systems you choose with the process and tools that you will use here.

I know! I know! A month??? Goodness that smacks of a commitment. Where's the instant transformation?? Pen and paper—good Lord! I ask, what's your hurry? This is a fun, exciting, amazing, profound journey—Do you wish away your vacation so that you can return to work? NO! You savor every moment of it. If you do the same here the result will be an experience that will begin to change your view of life and your role in creating it. Like everything else here, one week for each FBS is only suggestive, a starting point, the tip of the iceberg. This is really a continual, exciting journey. You will get started here with the basics and as your meditation practice matures and changes your exploration of your FBS will grow as well.

God

OK, time to start your first week of vacation and visit your FBS about God. OH GOD! Our FBS about God or a Higher Power or The Universe—whatever term you choose—is THE BIG ONE. Think of this one as the soil from which each of the other three spring forth. Eventually, you'll see how this one influences the other three and the many other smaller ones so don't miss a thing on this first week of vacation.

The only assumption I will make is that you believe in some sort of God, Higher Power, etc. Because you may have already spent a great deal of time exploring and determining the answers throughout your life you may be tempted to pass over the questions with quick answers. Resist that temptation and spend the time here too. Elaborate on your answers and push yourself for details. Exploring them with someone is also a good way to fully examine what you believe. If you are exploring the questions with someone, share your reasoning with them. Seeing your beliefs in front of you, hearing them, will take them from being thoughts to becoming Word.

Remember, this is your FBS. Rushing through your understanding of it is like trying to build the foundation for a home without laying the plans down on paper. Take your time and get it right.

Because of the differences between people's beliefs about a higher power their experiences will differ too. If your concept is of a Patriarchal Omnipotent Being and someone else's is of a formless energy that pulses through everything, the two of you will have different experiences. A concept of a Mother Goddess lays the groundwork for creating and relating to life in a much different way than the belief that God is Nature. The belief that you *are* God creates another experience, as does the belief that there are many Gods.

The following commonly held beliefs about God (pg. 123) and the accompanying exercises will help you begin to recognize and understand your beliefs about God. Now, at first glance, the beliefs may appear to be geared only towards people who hold more 'traditional' ideas and beliefs. If the word God is distracting for you then cross it out and put one in that works for you. Substituting the words "The Universe" or "The Divine" show that the statements also apply to metaphysical, New Age and Eastern beliefs too.

As an example, let's take a closer look at statement # 12 from pg. 125: **If I worship God then bad things will rarely happen to me.**

The key is to dig into the question and consider the root belief. The root belief here seems to be that you have to *do something* in order to *get something* you want or at least a favorable result. What is that?

If you have a less traditional idea of God you might say, *"Oh, well, I believe that I create my reality. I don't have to worship God in order to prevent bad things from happening to me."* In the case of a more metaphysical belief system it might be a certain way of thinking. The *create/co-create* my reality belief systems can sometimes have <u>requirement</u> worded this way, *"Disease is the result of negative (wrong) thinking. If I think the right way my illness will heal."* From a more traditional perspective it may be worship or attending religious services. If you are 'doing' those things, what does it mean if you don't get what you want or expect?

- Are you being punished?

- Denied?

- Doing it wrong?

- Is that just the way it is?

Another thing to consider when moving through the questions and statements along with the daily meditations are when you say you believe one thing but your actions belie a different belief. For example, do you say you believe that you create your own reality but find yourself asking God to change things when they are not the way you want them to be? This demonstrates that you'd like to believe that you create your reality but actually you believe that God does. Your belief is not congruent with your action. Or maybe you really believe in Co-Creation?

Remember, BELIEFS drive decisions and create EXPERIENCE. Your relationship with God is THE relationship, THE EXPERIENCE.

STOP for a much needed caveat ☺ There is a lot of intellectualizing going on here and necessarily so. But please bring intuition, prayer, Faith and spiritual consciousness to all of this. These ethereal, vague, and sometimes ambiguous energies and perspectives are what help you use your mind and thoughts as the tools they are intended to be. Feel the process. Feel the answers. Feel the experience of coming to know YOU deeper. Laugh. Have fun. Smile. Approaching it this way will prevent you from getting bogged down in the words and thoughts and ironically just creating chatter when what you want to do is get beneath it.

Daily Exercises

The following exercises are to be used in conjunction with the belief statements beginning on page 123. Each morning will have its own meditative exercise. But, each evening, you will have this same meditation:

Repetitive Evening Meditation: Sit comfortably with your back supported and your head tilted ever so slightly upward as if you are looking towards a spot just above the horizon. Close your eyes and breathe deeply and fully. Imagine meeting your God.

Day 1

Set your timer or alarm clock for 15 minutes, sit in a comfortable chair, close your eyes and breathe slowly and deeply. Place your hand on your chest to ensure that you are using your diaphragm to pull your breath all the way down into your lungs with minimal movement in your chest. Sit quietly, not opening your eyes and breathing until your timer goes off. Then, read the statements regarding God (pg. 123) with your morning coffee or whatever your morning routine. Take the book with you, tear the list out of the book or make a copy-just take the list with you. Re-read it throughout your day; at lunch, on the subway, standing in line at the grocery store, over dinner, at bedtime. As tempting as it may be to answer these today—don't. Just let them simmer. Allow the feelings and experiences that happen from just reading them come to the surface with repeated readings. Savor and ponder them.

Day 2

This morning during a 15 minute breathing meditation say the word "God" or "Higher Power" or "Goddess" or whatever term appeals to you on each exhale—out loud or to yourself. Remember to use your diaphragm and pull your breath all the way down into your lungs. Breathe in through your nose and out through your mouth. Keeping your eyes closed. Observe your thoughts and images as you say your mantra. When your alarm goes off open your eyes and sit quietly for a few more minutes—holding the idea of God in your consciousness. Then move into your day with your list in hand. As you read them today, highlight the ones that you feel sure you know your answers to. Then use another color to highlight those that you need to think about, dig into.

Day 3

What color did you highlight those statements that you felt sure you knew the answers to? As you get seated comfortably, set your timer and close your eyes. I want you to imagine that color. First the hue; on each exhale see different shades of that color, different intensities. Then start to imagine things that are that color--flowers, clothing, buildings, animals, etc. How does the color feel? What emotions and feelings do the images illicit? Remember to breathe deeply, in through your nose and out through your mouth. After your timer goes off sit quietly for a few minutes longer. Throughout the day, notice things that are this color. Read only those questions highlighted in this color. Read them, consider them, and consider what is at the root of the statement. Do not write anything down....yet.

Day 4

After your 15-minute meditation, fully respond to each of the statements that you meditated upon and considered yesterday. You don't have to write a book, but do be thorough. You may not have the time this morning to respond to all of them. So, carry your list with you and add to your answers throughout the day.

Day 5

This morning, during your meditation, imagine and concentrate on the color that you used for the statements that you needed to think about, dig into. First the hue; on each exhale see different shades of that color, different intensities. Next, things that are that color--flowers, clothing, buildings, animals, etc. How does the color feel? What emotions and feelings do the images illicit? Remember to breathe deeply, in through your nose and out through your mouth. Throughout the day take notice of things that are that color. Read only those questions highlighted in this color. Read them, consider them, and determine what is at the root of the statement.

Day 6

After your 15-minute meditation fully answer each of the questions that you meditated on and considered yesterday. You don't have to write a book, but do be thorough. So, carry your list of questions with you and add to your answers, thoughts and insights throughout the day.

Day 7

During your 15-minute meditation, repeat the word WHY on each exhale. Afterwards, begin by asking "Why" to your answers. A simple "No, I do not believe in a higher power" is not a foundation; it is simply the primary material for your foundation. Conclusions and perspectives will take that raw material and shape it into your FBS and then you can use it to understand your other belief systems. Again, carry your list with you throughout your day and jot down insights, elaborations and conclusions.

Seven days, one FBS. This time frame is purely suggestive and just a starting point. You may decide and need more time on any of these steps. You may want to go back and move through the process again. Meditate, ponder and consider each step and answer every question thoroughly and you will be wonderfully surprised at the awareness that you gain.

Beliefs about God

1. What is your concept of a higher power? Is it an unseen force or energy, a divine being, a human type figure or some other concept?

Really visualize how you VIEW God from a perspective of physical and see-able attributes. When you IMAGINE God—what do you see? If you sense God---what do you sense? If you believe that God Is EVERYTHING, does that mean inanimate/nonliving things too?

2. Does God have gender?

If you believe God is female, consider your relationship with the women in your life and your attitudes towards women in general? The same if you visualize God as male. Both genders? No gender?

3. Does God's favor have to be earned by doing something correct?

On the surface this one may seem fairly clear-cut. However, what about more subtle ways you may believe and act as if you have to earn God's approval such as— "I must value all life." This is not to say that valuing life is in any way not a good thing. This can also be "to remain in line with The Universe" It may be not doing 'bad' things or by doing 'good things'.

4.   Are you and God one in the same or separate?

Made in the image and likeness of God? Made of the same stuff as God. Completely different?

5.   How do you communicate with God?

Prayer, meditation, casual conversations, mantras, non-verbal sort of implied communication?

6.   Does God have expectations of you?

Are you expected to be good? To help the needy? Save the planet? These are things that you don't get extra credit for, you're just supposed to do them or be them.

7.   Where does God reside? Where is God?

In heaven—what is heaven? Where is it? Does God live among us? In you? Everywhere?

8.   Why doesn't God stop bad things from happening? Why do bad things happen in the Universe?

Dive deep on this one and be very open about what you believe. Just as we come to know people by what they do, we also come to know God by what we think God does or doesn't do.

9. Does The Universe punish you for wrongdoing or choices?

No? Why not? Yes? Why?

10. Does God communicate with you? How does God communicate with you?

If NO—then why not? If so, is it through ancient texts? A religious organization? Does he talk to you? Through pictures? Movies? Music?

11. God requires certain actions from us: obedience, worship, recognition, service, proselytizing, love, and respect.

Similar to #s 3 and 6 with a slant towards what you believe God may want from you from a one on one relationship.

12. If I worship God then bad things will rarely happen to me.

Karma is an example of this outside of traditional Western ideas. "Why did this happen to me?!"

13. There are many Gods.

Do they 'work' together? Is one of them 'in charge'? What do they do and why is there more than one? If you answer no...why not ☺ ?

14. What do you believe your relationship to this higher
power is?

Subordinate? Equal? Symbiotic? Parent/child?

15. Were you created sinful of perfect? Perfectly sinful?
*What does it mean to be sinful or perfect? Why would we be created one
way or another?*

For Notes, Thoughts and Ponderings

Now What?

So, what do you do with all of your new insights, considerations and answers about God? Well, now its time to figure out how they are *creating* in your life. Let's take two of the statements and determine how holding certain beliefs may create in your daily life.

#10 Does God communicate with you? How does God communicate with you?

Suppose you answered some version of *'through ancient texts'*. What experiences might this create in your relationship with God and in less direct ways in your daily life? Well, first, ancient manuscripts are ancient. This is also a belief that says

God has pretty much said whatever he has needed to say, quite a while ago. Tag onto this "the Bible, the Koran, the I Ching", or whatever text you look to, "has the answers and communication from God". Usually, this is also paired with the idea that God does not communicate directly with us anymore because it is all out there.

What does it feel like for you when someone says, "I have said all I have to say?" What is the experience for you? Frustration? Hurt? Anger? Maybe you feel the excitement of the challenge that the 'answers are there'! Gratitude? My guess is that many of us feel the first set of experiences.

On the surface, pouring through and exploring these texts may satisfy you spiritually and your desire to be close to God. You keep plugging away and maybe even find a sense of contentment with the answers and how they apply to your life. The underlying current may be different. Experiencing God as having 'said all there is to say' can leave you with a lot of questions and even a since of abandonment.

Imagine a loved one acting similarly. Refusing to further explain something to help you understand. You may eventually come to terms with this attitude. It doesn't cripple your life but it is always on the periphery. This can impact how you interact with others too.

If you hold this belief, when things happen in your life that are challenging, you may wonder how some of the outdated language and ideas of ancient texts relate to you. You might feel that you have somehow missed the answers. You may need to hear from God NOW!

As mentioned earlier, you attract people, situations and circumstances into your life that mirror your beliefs. What are you creating and attracting into your life with a belief that God only communicates through ancient texts? Do many people you encounter in your life have an "I have said all I have to say!" attitude? Maybe you have that attitude. Do you continually find yourself in circumstances that are rigid and only seem to have convoluted solutions?

You can live life believing that God is finished communicating, but suppose you believe that God is **also** communicating with you right here and now through modern writings as well. How does adding that belief create a different experience? Imagine the experience of going through your day knowing that God may communicate with you. Well, suddenly you experience that God is saying, *"I am still talking to you. I realize that some of this is difficult so I am trying to explain it in a way that makes sense to you where you are NOW."* Suddenly, you have the experience of being valued. Maybe you experience Faith that you are not alone 'in this'. You have the experience of having God right now. This feels like security, a sense of possibilities. What might this new belief attract and create in your life? Friends and family that are more open minded? Maybe you would be more patient when explaining things to people. Perhaps the answers about your purpose in life would seem possible and accessible.

Rarely will you have just one or two beliefs like these examples. Beliefs are usually a mix of several ideas rolled into one. But, one of them is usually more dominate than the others. It is the one that you fall back on. Also, no beliefs are wrong. What you are doing here is discovering yours and recognizing the experiences that they are creating. This is not all about trying to create only positive experiences. Remember, some 'negative' experiences later reveal themselves to be 'positive'.

Now, #15 Were you created sinful or perfect? Perfectly sinful?

This is a fascinating one. Consider what is at the root of this question. On the surface it might seem to apply primarily to people who hold more traditional beliefs about God. Judeo-Christian, Islamic and Buddhist beliefs all hold some clear element of this idea of being created sinful or imperfect.

And many people who hold these beliefs are OK with them. We'll get to that ☺

But, first, you New Thought folks are not out of the woods. Let's expand on SIN and see where you may be holding some belief about being created sinful or imperfect.

Sin is an archery term which means 'to miss the mark'. It has come to mean flawed or inherently less than, a moral or ethical defect, somehow not whole, in need of redemption. You get the idea.

CAVEAT: This is not a theological debate, just a broad definition and general usage of the term.

Any belief that says you are moving toward perfection naturally holds the idea that you are imperfect. A belief that life is a journey through the Universe, over and over again working towards perfection with each incarnation says that you are imperfect. I know that sounds a bit like Karma, and it does, because the New Thought movement has co-opted many aspects of Karmic teachings, so I am using it here. More modern ideas that are SIN reinvented are put forth as "Your dark side has to be transcended." "Some people are evil." "The EGO is dangerous and out to get you."

NEEDED CAVEAT: Remember, this is about discovering what is at the root of your beliefs. NOWHERE in this process is there a right and wrong, positive or negative. You are simply being guided to understanding how what you believe creates your experiences of life. A belief that you are sinful is not a wrong belief any more than believing that you are perfect is a right one. Each creates its own experiences, each of which are of value.

OK, back to Sin. Believing that you are inherently flawed can create positive experiences, especially when it is coupled with the idea that the imperfection has an ultimate purpose. Something that builds character, similar to how water shapes rock over a period of time. I think it was Michelangelo who said that David was in the marble all along; he just removed what wasn't David. By the way, the piece of marble used to create Michelangelo's masterpiece was considered by other sculptors to be too flawed for sculpting use. You thought I was going to start on the 'negative' end didn't you?

What if you simply believe that you were created or came into existence flawed, imperfect in a way that is 'bad'? Hmmmm. This could create experiences of self-loathing, the sense that nothing you do will ever be good enough or an undercurrent of feeling unloved or unlovable. Broken? Maybe when you are feeling sad and depressed you believe that it can't be improved because you were born that way. Beliefs that require some sort of redemption fall into this category.

What if you believe that you were created perfect? That you are perfectly flawed so to speak? That everything about you is exactly as it should be? Sounds great---on the surface. But, what might be an underlying current of such a belief? Most likely your experiences are somewhere in between or maybe you even vacillate between these examples. The object is to determine where your proverbial pendulum usually swings regarding the ideas of perfection, sin, imperfection, inherent flaws, etc. Use these examples as just an idea for how to dig deeper into the statements and questions.

I've helped you look deeper at two of the questions and, as you can see, there are many possibilities. The challenge is to pull them all together so you get an overview or a snap shot of what you believe about God. While doing so, be honest with yourself about all of them. It tends to be a badge of honor to be able to say, *"I believe in a totally loving and just God or Universe."* And maybe some of you do believe that; more times than not you hold a few beliefs that are counter to this.

Take a piece of paper and number it like the next page. Or if you own this book just use the next page. The list shortens each of the common beliefs to one or two words. Place your detailed list (the one that you wrote YOUR beliefs on) beside this one and then beneath each concept write the experiences that your beliefs create. To give you an idea of how this might work, I have written in possible experiences based on the two examples that we just considered.

Reread how I looked into #10 **Does God communicate with you? How does God communicate with you?** I decided that if I held similar beliefs as in the example, that God only communicates to me through ancient texts, that I might experience any of the following--frustration, hurt, anger, abandonment, excitement, curiosity. So, that's what I put under #10 on my list.

This step of the process is about forming a picture of what you believe and ultimately what you create. Remember, this isn't about finding the 'negative'. Balance what you put in here with both negative and positive when it is present. Both are almost always present ☺

1. Concept
2. Gender
3. Earn
4. One/Separate
5. Communicate to
6. Expectations
7. Reside
8. Bad Things
9. Punishment
10. Communication from
- Frustration, Hurt, Anger, Abandonment, Excitement, Curiosity
11. Requirement
12. Worship
13. Many Gods
14. Relationship
15. Sinful/Perfect
- Sad, Depressed, Unworthy, at Ease, Comforted

What kind of picture emerges when you get all of your beliefs about God in one place? You can even take a sheet of paper and make two columns—one negative, one positive-- and divide up your experiences. Where's the balance? What beliefs do you need to change in order to create an ultimately more positive experience in your relationship with God?

Changing God

Changing a component of a Belief System requires you to set down the belief that you want to change. You don't have to toss it out, just set it down long enough to consider what a new belief would create in your life. Examine it long enough to see if the new belief resonates and feels comfortable with you. You've already done half the work by discovering what you do believe.

Suppose you believe something similar to our example of question #10 and want to change a few things. Maybe change to a belief that says *God communicates through modern texts too and even movies or songs or other people.* Six steps, followed patiently, consistently and with openness will start the process.

1. IMAGINE that God is communicating with you.

You can use your Town Center for this! Get settled in a comfortable chair or on the couch and slip beneath the chatter with any of the tools and exercises you have learned about and used here already. Or using a new way you have discovered. Once your mind has become quieter and you are in a more meditative state take to the streets of your Town. As you move through the town, maybe on your way to the park, imagine that God is walking with you. Ask her how she will be communicating with you now that you are open to new ways of receiving communication. You can even ask for help changing your beliefs. Be sure to listen for the reply.

Go to the Mercantile or General Store and purchase a pair of Communication-Ray glasses that allow you to walk around your town and see the many ways that God is communicating with you. Or, take the glasses to the Cinema. Once there, have the projectionist play a movie of the past few days of your real life. With the glasses on you will be able to see all of the ways and times that God has communicated with you.

2. READ books, WATCH movies, LISTEN to music and SPEAK to people that share this new belief.

This one is easy to get started with. Go to the library or a book store and ask the Librarian or bookseller for books on communication from God. Visit a movie theater or search movie databases on line. You need a flood of new ideas, of new possibilities. Many people have shared their experiences of receiving communication from God in inspiring and thoughtful ways. Hearing their stories can open your heart and mind. Like replacing an inactive lifestyle with an active, healthier one, changing a belief means replacing it with one that is better suited for you. I'll make a couple of suggestions here, but a short perusal of any of the above places will wield lots of material.

- Conversations With God by Neale Donald Walsch actually everything by NDW.
- Trust Your Vibes by Sonia Choquette
- Lifeline (CD) by Iris Dement
- Shaina Noll (CD) Songs for the Inner Child
- Waiting for Autumn by Scott Blum
- Caroline Myss-any of her audio programs

3. LOOK for communication from God.

As you go through your day notice when you have just the right experience or hear just the right encouragement. Try speaking to God throughout your day. Ask to be aware how and when he is communicating with you. Notice when your heart flutters with 'It is me, communicating with you." Be open. Tell yourself to be open. Use the talking to your mind exercise and discipline your mind with love and patience to accept a new belief and experience.

4. On a daily basis, give yourself PERMISSION to believe something new.

Simply tell yourself, " I give myself permission to believe that God communicates with me."

5. Meditate through-out your day

Use meditation to get beneath the chatter daily, even several times daily. Use the tools and exercises that we have learned here. They are practical and designed to be USED all day, any day. Contemplate and meditate on Communication from God. Only when you are beneath the chatter can you truly learn to listen and hear God. Eventually it will become second nature. But in the beginning it takes a little work.

6. JOIN Social groups, coffee shops, gatherings and spiritual organizations.

Join a book study group, Yoga class or spiritual organization. Meet people who share the belief that you want to create and accept. Hang out at the local, independent coffee shop. You know the funky ones with the used furniture and kitschy lamps and nick' knacks. Have a cup of coffee, sit and read for a while.

Seems like a lot of time, energy and effort? It is. You didn't form and cement your current beliefs over night or with ease. It just seems that way because you weren't doing it consciously. It won't take years to change them because you have just added consciousness to the process!

These steps can be used to further explore and change any belief you choose. Just substitute the belief you want to change for *Communication from God* and you have the perfect outline for changing another belief that may not serve you.

The importance of spending continual time understanding your beliefs about God cannot be understated. Every belief you have, every decision you make, every action you take and every experience you have in life stems from your beliefs about your higher power. While I have laid out a system that has worked for others and me, it's only suggestive and certainly not THE comprehensive way to discover and understand these beliefs and the experiences they create.

I'm just attempting to get you moving, thinking and inspired. It doesn't end with this chapter and it is not restricted to the ideas and suggestions contained here. Take the ball and run with it. On a daily basis, question yourself, talk to God, be open and be willing to try new ways of thinking. Imagine possibilities. Finally, do more than intellectualize—meditate, pray, use your intuition as a way of living.

Death

Of the four Foundational Belief Systems, Death can be the most challenging for you to look at more closely. There are a lot of fears and uncertainty imbedded in beliefs about death. Even people with tremendous Faith in their idea of God can have a very difficult time moving through the fears wrapped up in their beliefs about death. At times there can even be clear contradictions between what someone says they believe about God and what they believe about Death. Also, an interesting and subtle difference between the two FBS is that God is an entity and Death is an event. So, how you dig deeper to the following statements and beliefs will probably have less of a relationship feel and more of a *relate to feel*. You'll see what I mean very soon.

You'll take a closer look at Death in the same manner that you did with God. Remember, the statements are only suggestive, a starting point to get you considering. I liken it to the old saying 'stirring the pot'. As with the statements about God, work to discover the core belief or idea behind each of them. If you quickly dismiss one, then I suggest you spend more time on that one.

Pendulum Exercise

With much fear wrapped up in this FBS, getting in there and stirring the pot may likely bring a lot of it to the surface. You may find yourself feeling anxious, sad, or nervous. When this happens, close your eyes, breathe deeply, and become quieter. Once you are below the nervous and fearful chatter imagine a pendulum that is swinging between two points. One point is fear and the other is faith. Each time you exhale imagine the pendulum moving away from Fear and towards Faith. If you prefer, you can use God instead of Faith. Continue breathing deeply, moving the pendulum away from fear. Recognizing that fear is there but choosing to move away from it for now. You may have to do this often as you work through this FBS. By the time you are finished you will become aware of the beliefs that are causing so much fear.

You will use the same meditative exercises that you used with your FBS of God on pages 118-122. I suggest you photocopy those and the following common beliefs regarding Death and carry both lists with you. Remember, you will be pondering, highlighting and deciding about these statements for the next week.

Here is Day 1 to get you started.

Day 1

Set your timer or alarm clock for 15 minutes, sit in a comfortable chair, close your eyes and breathe slowly and deeply. Place your hand on your chest to ensure that you are using your diaphragm to pull your breath all the way down into your lungs with minimal movement in your chest. Sit quietly, not opening your eyes and breathing until your timer goes off. Then, read the statements regarding Death with your morning coffee or whatever your morning routine. Take the book with you, tear the list out of the book or make a copy-just take the list with you. Re-read it throughout your day; at lunch, on the subway, standing in line at the grocery store, over dinner, at bedtime. As tempting as it may be to answer these today—don't. Just let them simmer. Allow the feelings and experiences that happen from just reading them come to the surface with repeated readings. Savor and ponder them.

Death Beliefs and Statements

1. Death is the end.

WOW! I figured you better start out the gate with the big one. Most of you will say, "No. no. Can't be. But I don't know what comes after it." Well, no one who hasn't gone there knows for sure. Do you in some degree fear that death may be all there is?? Even if it is just 'maybe' 'slightly'?? My experience is that we all hold some bit of this belief. What's your %?

2. God takes people when it is their time.

All major religions and spiritual traditions have some element of this belief. God or The Universe determines when you die. Many times you have no issue with God taking you. But, when she takes your child or Mother......hmmm.

3. You choose when you die.

In less traditional belief structures and New Thought beliefs this is very common. Right away there is the sense of control and relief at holding this belief. Like number two above, this seems to be OK for YOU. But a whole different experience is created when your loved one 'chooses' to die.

Are you only choosing to die when it is peaceful and surrounded by loved ones? What about car crashes, being murdered or killed in a hurricane?

4.   Suicide is never acceptable.

Obvious suicide vs. the slow and easy way with say drugs, alcohol or tobacco. Is there a difference? Can suicide really exist if God takes people when their time is up? If it is OK to take your own life what experience does that create?

5.   Death is never easy.

If you hold this belief or one similar, what experience does having it 'hang over your head' create? One of impending pain and sorrow? Dread?

6.   We grow old and die because we are physically imperfect and spiritually deficient.

This one is similar to our beliefs about Sin. And again, holding this belief is neither positive nor negative.

7.   It is more of a loss when someone young dies as opposed to someone old.

It is often said that the loss of a child is the worse loss anyone can experience. Well, what if you don't have children but you loose your spouse or a sibling? What if your child dies but you feel as if the loss is manageable?

8. Cremation is a sin.

What IS your belief about what should be done with your body after you die? Does it matter? Why does it matter?

9. Grief and sadness when a loved one dies shows lack of faith in God or life beyond death.

This is another one that seems so 'easy' on the surface. Why doesn't my Faith sustain me? Feelings of guilt because you are sad may be masking this belief.

10. Good people die because God wants them to come home/Bad people die as punishment.

Somewhere, somehow God is doing the 'dying' ☺ *Maybe Karma? Something other than you or the person dying is making the choice, causing the death.*

11. At death, our souls go before God who decides whether we go to heaven to be with Him or go to hell to be tortured forever.

Some belief systems couch this as a 'Life Review' that occurs before we move on to the next life. Look for beliefs that require you or God to pass judgment or assess your life.

12. Without the certainty of death we would not appreciate life.

There is fear in this belief but also gratitude and perspective. Knowing the certainty of Death. Also, maybe there is the idea that you are not grateful without Death looming over you.

13. With enough faith we could prevent the death of our physical bodies.

Given that everyone dies you would think that this one is silly and that no one holds this belief. Many of us do.

14. Life should be extended by any means possible-- prayer, medicine, and machines.

Maybe you hold this belief some of the time. If so, what makes you shift to a belief of not extending 'by an means possible'?

Now What?

Take a piece of paper and number it like page 155. Or if you own this book just use the next page. This list shortens each of the beliefs to one or two words. Place your detailed list, containing the answers you've written, beside this one and then beneath each concept/idea write the experiences that your beliefs create. You did this with the God statements. Remember, this isn't about finding the 'negative'. Balance what you put in here with both negative and positive, when they are both present. Both are almost always present ☺ It is about forming a picture of what you believe and ultimately what you create.

Let's look at two of the belief statements together and determine how their entries might be filled in on page 155:

9. Grief and sadness when a loved one dies shows lack of faith in God or life beyond death.

For the sake of our example, let's assume that you believe the statement just as it is written.

Guilt: Everyone experiences sadness and grief when a loved one dies. Those feelings are part of the natural process of loss. When you believe, as #9 states, that this natural process shows a lack of faith, then Guilt is created because 'your faith is not strong enough' or 'God must be disappointed because you don't believe in His promises'.

Disappointment or Confusion: For those of you with metaphysical and New Age viewpoints, maybe you experience disappointment or confusion that your beliefs about 'creating your own experience' don't seem to be working in this case. "Why can't I create acceptance and happiness when my loved one has gone on to the next part of her journey?"

Inspired and Curious: On the positive end of the spectrum, perhaps this example belief may create Inspiration and Curiosity by causing you to wonder how your Faith in God can be changed or applied in a new way that brings you comfort during the grieving process.

3. You choose when you die.

Empowered and Responsible: Anytime that we feel we have a say in anything we usually feel some bit of empowerment. With that empowerment comes responsibility.

On some level, we may experience anger at ourselves if we are not ready to die.

Blame: The other side of this is when loved ones die. If on some level our loved one chooses to die, we might blame them for leaving.

These two examples are approached from a very simple perspective in order to demonstrate how to consider what experiences your own beliefs may create. Be sure to consider both the 'positive' and 'negative' and be honest and balanced with yourself as to what experiences your beliefs create. You may find in many cases that both some positive and negative is created.

CAVEAT: Remember, so called negative experiences can be normal and healthy depending on the circumstances. Also, as mentioned previously, some experiences that were positive initially can turn out to be negative with the passage of time.

1. The End
2. Taken
3. Choose
- Empowered and Responsible. Or Blame
4. Suicide
5. Easy
6. Grow Old
7. Young vs. Older
8. Cremation
9. Grief
- Inspired and Curious. Or maybe Guilty and Confused
10. Home vs. Punishment
11. Heaven or Hell
12. Certainty, appreciation
13. Enough Faith
14. Extended

Just as you did with the God statements, take a piece of paper and create two columns--Negative and Positive. Take your created experiences from the list on page 153 and place them in the appropriate column. Remember, this isn't about finding the 'negative'. Balance what you put in here with both negative and positive when it is present. Both are almost always present ☺ It is about forming a picture of what you believe and ultimately what you create. I suggest taking a few days to meditate on all of the beliefs, feelings and experiences that you have navigated before moving forward.

A Different Death

As I said before, this one is challenging and with good reason. After sitting with the collective image for a couple of days, what sort of Experience Picture has emerged for you?

Changing beliefs within this system is about coming to terms with certainty and uncertainty. This involves not only the certainty of your own death but even more challenging, the certainty of the death of those whom you love. The beginning of facing this is fully acknowledging and accepting that death is certain for each person. While this is not specifically one of the statements it actually underpins a healthy understanding and formation of this FBS. The uncertain part is everything else ☺.

For certain you will die, as will everyone that you care about. As will everyone period. It seems like a no-brainer that this is true. The problem is that most people have not spent the thoughtful consideration needed to actually accept this fact due to the great deal of fear created by what they believe about death.

My guess is there will always be some level of fear surrounding death for each of us. It is only natural to fear the unknown and this is the BIG unknown. What you want to do is decrease the amount of fear that surrounds death. You now have many meditation tools to help you do just that.

The suggestions below will help you alleviate some of the fear surrounding death and change beliefs about death too. Just like you did with your FBS about God.

1. Try the following meditation for at least two weeks. Find a nice park to go to and meditate. Or if you have your own yard you can use it. Layout a blanket and pillow and lie down facing up toward the sky with your arms outstretched. Breathe deeply and slowly.

2. Use visualization. Go to your Town Center.
Go to the University and take a class on the aspects of
Death. Maybe attend a special class hosted by people who
have died.

3. READ books and WATCH movies that explore
    Death from a spiritual and positive, thought
    provoking perspective. Watch a documentary on
    Near-death Experiences
    • You Can't Afford The Luxury of A Negative
       Thought by Peter McWilliams
    • Death and Dying by Elisbeth Kubler Ross
    • What Dreams May Come (movie)

4. Talk to people who are willing to share their beliefs
    about death.
Not only their own death but the deaths of others. Many
people who have lost loved ones want to talk about the
experience. Consider how people's experiences (thus
beliefs) have shifted and changed over time regarding
death in general and specific deaths.

5. Visit a cemetery

Do this twice during the coming month. Death has been surgically removed from our society and culture. Prior to the 20th Century, most people died at home and were then buried in the family cemetery that was tended to by each generation. These visits will help you to fully accept and acknowledge the certainty of death. They will also inspire you to come to your own conclusions and beliefs about death.

6. Talk to God about Death and LOOK for communication from God about Death.

This is a simple one but always the thing that you forget to do ☺ Talk her ear off. Ask questions, listen for answers in the next conversation with a friend or the song on the radio or the dream that you have tonight. Ask for understanding and comfort.

7. On a daily basis give yourself PERMISSION to believe that Death is more than you currently understand it to be.

Who really knows what Death is and what happens when we die? Nobody. Absolutely nobody. No matter how authoritative someone may sound when talking about what death is, it is still just OPINION. You can accept someone else's belief about death or piece together your own from many sources. Or, you can create your own from thin air.

8. Volunteer

Volunteer at your local hospice or an organization that assists the terminally ill. Empathy and sympathy are tremendous catalysts for changing your beliefs about death and conquering your fears. You don't have to volunteer for direct patient care. You can file papers, answer phones or clean the facility. The purpose is to put you into an environment that faces death each day with compassion, empathy and strength; an environment that strips away some of the taboo of speaking about death and the mystery of dying.

There is only one true fact regarding Death—everyone will die. Yes, there are many interesting ideas and suppositions and speculations about this major life event...explore them. But, no matter how enlightened or informed anyone may seem to be, THEY DO NOT KNOW any TRUTH beyond the fact that we all die. Everything else regarding Death is BELIEF. You get to choose what you believe and then experience about death. Never forget that. And, please don't stop here but work to allow your beliefs to expand and evolve. Allow them to be what YOU CHOOSE them to be not what someone else has determined.

What about Material Security and Sexuality?

With God and Death you tend to leave people alone or at least just shake your head and move on. But with Material Security and Sexuality you have a lot of ideas about other people's money and what they should or should not be doing with it; and especially with whom they should or should not be doing **what** with, with their own body. It is almost as if there is a sub-FBS that you have to work through that involves 'other people's Sex and Money' .

The advantage to all of this busy-bodyness is that it makes it easier for you to recognize commonly held beliefs about Money and Sex because you have spent a lot of time 'being nosey'. Just remember that your judgments are beliefs that define you and create experience.

CAVEAT TIME: As before, this is a lot of intellectualizing. Now, marry that intellectualizing with experience by using your meditation practice, intuition, prayer, visualization and get beneath the chatter of Material Security and Sexuality. Don't be so serious! Have fun!

Material $ecurity

Beliefs about Material Security, like those about Death, have a lot of fear wrapped up in them. That fear has as much to do with not having enough as it does with having too much. From an everyday perspective to a spiritual one, your FBS about Material Security can run roughshod over the other three if you are not careful. But, like the other three FBS, once you take a closer and more conscious look at your beliefs about Material Security you will begin to change some of them and release the fears associated with them.

Ask yourself, "What is material security?" Defining this is different than discovering what brings you a feeling of security. If someone acquires a great deal of 'material security', but lives in constant fear of losing it, is what they have acquired material security? Is security being free from worry and concern? Does it provide you with a sense of safety and contentment? Does security come from within you, or from having certain conditions outside of you? A combination of both? What is that perfect balance for you?

From an everyday perspective, your beliefs about material security and money drive many of your decisions and create some of your most powerful experiences. *'What to do when you have no money?'* **and** *'What to do with it when you do have it?'*, is one of many dilemmas that surfaces in beliefs about material security. In addition to 'cash flow' there are the many things which you believe you need in order to feel secure. You put a lot of stock in these things (pun intended).

Next is how your spirituality and your relationship with God figures into this FBS. There are a lot of commonly held beliefs about money and material security that are in direct conflict with what many of you are striving for in terms of a spiritually fulfilling life and your relationship with God. And then there are the moral and ethical ideas about the supposed responsibilities that come attached to abundance of any type.

This FBS is usually tied to and affects your self-esteem and self-image. A great deal of this influence has to do with your assumption that everyone else is judging you in this area in much the same way that you may be judging them ☺

You may also tend to do a lot to justify your worry and fear where security and money is concerned. "Well, I have to make a living!", "If I don't worry about it how will I pay my bills?", "Easy for you to say because you have a nice home and know that your next paycheck will cover the mortgage." You may also sometimes justify why others don't have enough. *"They are lazy."*, *"This is the land of opportunity."*, *"Get a job."*, *"Live within your means."* Judgment and justification are BIG in this FBS.

I have created a slightly different system for you to use to explore Material Security. It will still include lots of meditation and visualization and a set of commonly held beliefs. However, the common Material Security beliefs will be opposing beliefs. The reason for the change is that I want you to have more than one way of exploring Beliefs. So, if one does not appeal to you or you find one not as effective, you have a back-up.

Let's get Going….

A No Money Week: While you explore your Material Security FBS, you are going to have a 'no money' week to help you realize how much time, energy and effort you spend preoccupied with money—getting it, spending it, not spending it, using it to impress others or to distract yourself from feelings you don't want to feel and to influence or control other people.

I want you to experience that you don't need money EVERY minute of EVERY day. It may surprise you to recognize that most days you have EVERYTHING you need without acquiring one additional thing. Without spending one more dollar. I want you to see that much of your energy is spent in no man's land when it comes to money—THE FUTURE.

For the next week do not spend any money. That includes cash, credit cards, gift certificates, store credits, etc. To get ready for this challenge fill up your car, buy your bus pass that is about to expire, go to the grocery store and move anything off your schedule that may require you to spend. This includes dinner dates, movies, theater, concerts and morning stops for coffee.

During this week you are not going to pay any bills or deal with financial affairs. So more planning is needed. If you pay your bills online, schedule them now. Do you pay bills by check? Make them out now for the bills that are due during the coming week, write the date that each needs to be mailed on the back of each envelope and put stamps on the envelopes. You may drop them in the mail according to the date on the envelope. That is the only money thing you are allowed to do during the coming week. Finally, you're not allowed to tell anyone that you are having a No Money Week.

OK, now that you are ready for your No Money Week it is time for you to spend that week with your Material Security FBS.

This time around I have offered opposing beliefs (beginning on page 178) for you to consider. My reasoning for this is that many of your beliefs about money and material security are extremes. By starting with a comparison you will be more able to determine where your beliefs reside. These are only a starting point. Your job, again, is to dig deep like you did with God and Death.

Take the first opposing statements for example:

Money is evil

Money is Good

You are probably more than willing to say that money is evil, the love of money is evil, the pursuit of material things is evil—or some version of this idea. Attributing negative characteristics to money and its influence is something that many people do.

Now, say to yourself 'Money is good.' Feels funny or false, doesn't it? Seem silly? When trying to attribute positive characteristics or qualities to money you probably throw a 'but only if....' qualifier on the end. Only if you give it away. Only if there is some altruistic value. Only if....

In this case, comparing the two beliefs may help you to see how silly it is to consider money to be Good or Bad. Money can not have human characteristics. It is neutral. By digging deeper you will find that it is your relationship to money that is better labeled 'good' or 'bad'. Of course, more accurate labels might be 'useful' and 'not useful'. The point is to use the comparison beliefs to dig into WHAT YOU BELIEVE.

Another caveat needed: This is not an exercise in intellectualizing. It is an exercise in using your mind as the tool it is designed to be. The difference? You are using your mind in conjunction with meditation , your intuition and your sense of awareness. You have a specific task... *look at your life to see what you believe instead of looking to your thoughts to tell you.*

Meditations

Day 1, Morning

For 15 minutes, sit comfortably with your eyes closed and bring yourself into a meditative state using your breath and by saying the word Money. On your inhale say the first syllable "Mon". And on your exhale say the second syllable "ney'. While saying the mantra, imagine all of the forms money can take. Bills, coins, credit cards, checks, online accounts where you never lay hands on anything tangible. Visualize other ways that you exchange something for something you want or need; coupons, certificates, bartering, trading. When your 15 minutes is up, take your list of opposing beliefs (pg. 178) with you and read them throughout the day. Just mull them over; don't answer anything.

Day 1, Evening

15 minutes, Security Exists: Sit comfortably, close your eyes and breathe deeply through your nose, filling your lungs fully with each inhale. And fully emptying your lungs when exhaling through your mouth. Once your mind has quieted

and you feel as if you are getting beneath the chatter, say the following mantra:

With each inhale say: Security

With each exhale say: Exists

Day 2, Morning

During your 15 minute breathing meditation, I want you to place a sticker or a small piece of tape on your Third-Eye. This will help you focus your attention on that area. Also, instead of having your head tilted slightly downward (as people typically do when meditating) tilt your head slightly up so that your line of sight is just above the horizon. Be sure not to tilt it back so far that it is uncomfortable. Actually, just a slight nod upward will suffice. Once your mind has become quieter, imagine all of the 'things' which you believe would cause you to feel secure if you had them in your life. Remember to use your diaphragm and pull your breath all the way down into your lungs. Breathe in through your nose and out through your mouth. Keeping your eyes closed. A home, a car, money in the bank, a stable relationship? When your alarm goes off move into your day with your list in hand. As you read them today, highlight the ones that you feel sure you know 'where in between the two, your belief lies. Then use

172

another color to highlight those that you need to think about, dig into.

Day 2, Evening

15 minutes, I am content: Play a piece of classical music of your choosing. Many classical pieces are more than 15 minutes in length but you can also choose several smaller pieces if you wish. If own no classical music, go online and listen/download a piece that you find pleasing. I suggest you choose a piece that you are unfamiliar with or that you have no previous experiences attached to. While listening to the music, close your eyes and breathe. Follow the ebb and flow of the music and say the following mantra:

With each inhale say: I am

With each exhale say: content

Day 3, Morning

What color did you highlight the opposing beliefs that you felt sure you knew where your 'in between belief' was? As you get seated comfortably, set your timer and close your eyes. I want you to imagine that color. First the hue; on each exhale see different shades of that color, different intensities. Then start to imagine things that are that color--flowers, clothing, buildings, animals, etc. How does the color feel? What emotions and feelings do the images illicit? Remember to breathe deeply, in through your nose and out through your mouth. After your timer goes off sit quietly for a few minutes longer. Throughout the day, notice things that are this color. Read only those opposing beliefs that are highlighted in this color. Read them and consider what is at the root of these extremes and where your belief falls. Do not write anything down....yet.

Day 3, Evening
Use the Day 2, Evening meditation and mantra-I am content.

Day 4, Morning
After your 15-minute meditation, write down each of your beliefs that you meditated on and considered yesterday. You don't have to write a book but do be thorough. You may not have the time this morning to respond to all of them. Carry your list with you and add to your answers throughout the day.

Day 4, Evening
15 minutes, Facing a wall. Close your eyes and breathe deeply and fully, using your diaphragm. Meditation is almost always

practiced while facing out into a room or location. This exercise helps you to turn your attention and awareness inwards. Recognize how it feels in terms of your attention when you are facing the wall vs. the room. You may notice a more easily inward direction to your focus.

Day 5, Morning

This morning during your meditation imagine and concentrate on the color that you used for the opposing beliefs that you needed to think about, dig into. First the hue; on each exhale see different shades of that color, different intensities. Next, things that are that color--flowers, clothing, buildings, animals, etc. How does the color feel? What emotions and feelings do the images illicit? Remember to breathe deeply, in through your nose and out through your mouth. Throughout the day take notice of things that are that color. Read only those questions highlighted in this color. Read only those opposing beliefs that are highlighted in this color.

Day 5, Evening

Your choice: Choose one of the many meditations that you have used thus far. Or envision a new meditation. Be sure that you meditate for at least 15 minutes.

Day 6, Morning

After your 15-minute meditation, write down each of your beliefs that you meditated on and considered yesterday. You don't have to write a book, but do be thorough. Carry your list of questions with you and add to your answers, thoughts and insights throughout the day.

Day 6, Evening

Your choice: Choose one of the many meditations that you have used thus far. Or envision a new meditation. Be sure that you meditate for at least 15 minutes.

Day 7, Morning

During your 15-minute meditation, repeat the word Security on each exhale. Afterwards, carry your list with you throughout your day and jot down insights, elaborations and conclusions. Begin by asking "Why" to your beliefs. A simple "Yes, lots of money makes me feel secure." is not a foundation; it is simply the primary material for your foundation. Conclusions and perspectives will show you how that belief is creating experience in your life regarding security.

Day 7, Evening

Your choice: Choose one of the many meditations that you have used thus far. Or envision a new meditation. Be sure that you meditate for at least 15 minutes.

Material Security Opposing Beliefs

1. Money is evil.

   Money is Good.

2. To reach enlightenment I have to distance myself from money.

   I can wallow in money and still become enlightened.

In what ways do you believe 'having things' clouds enlightenment or awareness. Or do you think that just applies to other people? If you feel enlightened but have money do you feel like a sham? Do you judge spiritual teachers who have fancy cars?

3. If I have a lot of money then I am on the wrong path.

   The right path means very little material security.

Where are material security and money along your path. They are there. Where is your desire and need for them?

4. People who have material comforts and wealth have an obligation to give to those who have less.

Why should people have to give their money away?!

Follow this one closely—while many people expect the wealthy to donate a % of their income or feel obligated to donate a % of their own income they usually want to determine 'who' gets it. Or they donate but hold beliefs similar to #11.

5. Spiritual teachers should give their message for free or for a minimal fee to cover basic expenses.

    People only value what they pay for.

Do you hold beliefs that shun or outright oppose the exchange of money (profit) for spiritual materials, books, workshops and services? Outside of the box "Charitable donations should not be tax deductible."

6. We should only purchase and consume things that are necessary—food, clothing, and shelter.

    Spending money on lots of things helps other people meet their material needs.

What do you term responsible spending or accumulation of things? If people hoard, they are miserly. If you spend you are frivolous.

7. Material modesty is a must for religious individuals.

    In the Bible, Koran, Bhagavad Gita, etc., God showers his favorites with opulence.

Less traditional beliefs have this conundrum as well. New Thought spiritual writers and teachers are expected to be modest with their income that is generated by writing and speaking about abundance.

8. Financial security is obtainable.

There is no such thing as material security.

The old conundrum and conflict of the spiritual vs. the physical world. All is an illusion. Everything is real. I think Bill Gates has financial security, material security ☺

9. Homeownership provides security.

Homeownership is just renting from the bank.

If the bank can take it away, does your security really exist? When do you actually own a home?

10. There is not enough money to go around.

Money grows on trees.

Consider, in US paper currency alone, it is estimated that there is $850 BILLION dollars worth currently in circulation. Coins are another story as are all of the other currencies around the globe.

11. If you don't have enough material security its because your lazy or don't work hard enough.

Anyone with enough money has worked hard to get it.

Some people are lazy, yes. Some people don't work hard. The root of this belief is tied to any idea that money is a reward for hard work.

12. Tithing is required to get into heaven.

The streets of Heaven are paved with gold.

Many religious beliefs have some element of required or suggested giving in order to fund 'God's' work. Or is this just membership dues to a club?

13. Having a lot of money will corrupt you.

Money does not influence your character.

People with money can be corrupted by it, right? If that is the case then people without it seem to be corrupted by it as well as evidenced by their opinions of people with money? Hmmmm

14. Follow a spiritual path and your financial needs will disappear.

I have to take care of my material needs as consciously as I do my spiritual needs.

This is one of those REWARD beliefs. If I do something I get something in return. In this case, my material concerns will be taken care of. Where do you see money 'should be' a reward?

15. Insurance policies - life, auto, health, mortgage - guarantee security.

Buying insurance policies guarantees nothing except something you'll never be able to use.

Where in your life do you use money to buy more security in the form of more money. Can security be bought?

Now, using the list below and based on your newly recognized or articulated beliefs about Material Security, determine what experiences these beliefs may create for you in your life. You have done this twice before with God and Death. I suggest taking a couple of days to do this part and use your meditation practice frequently to help you arrive at the answers.

1. Evil/Good
2. Distance/Wallow
3. Right/Wrong Path
4. Obligation/No Obligation
5. Free/Charge
6. Spend/Don't Spend
7. Modesty/Opulence
8. Obtainable/Out of reach
9. Homeownership
10. Not Enough/Grows on Trees
11. Lazy/Hard Worker
12. Tithing/Heaven Has Enough
13. Corrupt/No Influence
14. Disappear/Take care of your own
15. Insurance Policies

Remember how you made a Positive/Negative sheet with God and Death? Do the same with your Material Security Beliefs and see which side of the page your beliefs tend to fall more often.

Discovering Security

1. Begin each day, recognizing what you do have in terms of security.

Do you have enough to eat and a safe place to sleep tonight? Are you confident that the same will be true tomorrow? Sound a bit cliché? There is great truth in many clichés. And that truth is usually overlooked or not valued. You have experienced how essential breathing is to a meditation practice and getting beneath the Chatter? Place the same importance on acknowledging, EACH DAY, that you have what you require. Gratitude.

2. Have a No Money day or week.

Think of this as fasting. Many spiritual practices advocate fasting as a way of purifying and raising awareness. No-Money time periods put you back in control rather than letting money run the show. They also allow you to CONSCIOUSLY interact with the energy of money in all of its forms.

3. Watch a movie, read a book or listen to music that inspires you. Do things that inspire you.

Feeling inspired, being inspired is a sure way to experience a sense of security. When you are inspired you are in many ways beneath the chatter of your every day mind and in touch with your TRUE self. Inspiration is a state of awareness and confidence, not only in yourself but in a larger picture.

- Read any writings by Martin Luther King Jr. A great collection of these is contained in A Testament of Hope, The Essential Writings and Speeches of Martin Luther King, Jr. Edited by James M. Washington. Be sure that you read Dr. King's writings and not someone's commentary and analysis of his writings.

- Visit the ocean, a lake, take a day trip to the country or the mountains. Get out in nature. If this is not possible, visit a city park or botanical gardens. Recognizing that you are part of NATURE not separate from it provides comfort and assurance.

- Spend as much time as you can with people who love and support you. And who make you laugh.

- If you have an MP3 player, create a play list of inspiring songs. Bring in songs from different genres.

I have a list that includes country, alternative rock, classic jazz and more; every song in the list has inspiring lyrics and music.

4. Bring down your debt

*   If you have debt, make a commitment to get it paid off. Mountains of debt can make you feel very insecure and overwhelmed. Don't waste time justifying the debt or bemoaning the weight of it. Determine how long it will take you to pay it off and mark off the months and years as you come closer to your goal. If it really is too much for you to overcome, talk to a lawyer and consider filing bankruptcy. Stay active with your debt. You didn't get there over night and you won't get out from underneath it quickly either.

5. Meditate and talk to your God

*   Whenever you are feeling insecure, meditate. Talk to your God. Ironically, it seems as though when we need meditation and conscious interaction with our Higher Power the most, we do neither. How long should you meditate or talk to your God? Until you feel better and in this case more secure.

6. Use your Town Center

- Use your breathing to meditate and get beneath the
  chatter and then go to your Town Center. Perhaps go
  to the Material Security Savings and Loan. This is a
  unique business that offers advice and loans out
  security. It is staffed by Security Experts who will
  evaluate your needs, based on your concerns, and you
  won't be turned down for any reason. Share with
  them all of your concerns, fears and hopes. And when
  you leave, take a big bag of assurance and sense of
  security.

There is a tremendous amount of outside pressure
regarding money and security, probably more so than with
God and Death. Much of it fear based. Thus, this FBS can be
quite a struggle to 'keep ahead of'. Remember, you get to
define what security means for you; where it comes from. Just
as with God and Death, the end of this chapter is only the
beginning for you. A sense of security will not be had from
reading this or any book. It is a process that grows and
evolves with your continued acceptance and understanding of
the circumstances in your inner and outer world.

Sexuality, What do you think?

Sexuality is a primary driving force in your life and your beliefs about it are very powerful. In terms of a FBS, Sexuality helps form your identity and self-concept and drives your relationships and views of others as well. As much as our more 'liberated' society may try to convince you that Sexuality is just Sex, there is much more creating your emotional, physical and spiritual experiences where Sexuality is concerned.

Part of diving deeper into Sexuality is getting past the physical act of sex and looking more broadly at your sexuality and sexual identity. Like the FBS you've already explored, this one will surprise you as you look closer. While Death may have elicited a lot of fear and anxiety, Beliefs about Sexuality can bring forth shame, embarrassment and even a sophomoric reaction. Finally, feelings of defensiveness and judgment will sometimes rise to the surface. You may be willing to give people their God and their very own Death but, you sometimes get a bit funny about their sexual identity. So, remember, this is about YOU and only YOU. Where you run into defensiveness and judgment meditate more deeply and look for the beliefs that are creating these experiences.

CAVEAT (yes, again) I am not putting myself out there as a behaviorist or a psychologist. I am just putting my observations and conclusions on the table as a starting point for you to discover your own.

So, for the sake of what you will do here, what is Sexuality? Sexuality encompasses your beliefs about gender identification, how you view and determine roles for men and women in relationship and society; your beliefs about sexual orientation, sexual behavior and societal norms along with how your spiritual beliefs dictate your own sexual behavior and judgment of others.

Generally, you think of sexuality in terms of the gender that you are attracted to sexually. These Sexuality beliefs determine your relationships with the gender that you are not attracted to as well. You will consider how your beliefs about sexuality influence your relationship with both genders.

For example, if you are a heterosexual man, your relationships with other men—friends, family, co-workers—are to some degree determined by your beliefs about sexuality and gender roles and how men should relate to one another.

How you view both sexes and their roles in the family and in society are wrapped up in-part with your beliefs about gender. What it means to be a woman or a man. Also, how early you expect boys and girls to assume those roles.

Sexuality will be different

Having spent much time on auto-pilot myself, I know how challenging it can be to begin to thoughtfully THINK and use meditation. My own experience has enabled me to learn tools that can be helpful in turning off the autopilot and the chatter, allowing the experience of more conscious and thoughtful thinking. With the previous FBS, I put a lot of suggestions, elaborations and ideas along with the statements for you to consider. I wanted to be sure that you were given examples and a thorough system for digging beneath the surface; to be sure to show you how deeper-thinking may appear. The meditative exercises and the system were laid out with that goal in mind; with a deliberate and steady pace that built upon each day's mediation, ponderings and answers. Stretching out your thought process and enabling you to come to see and know that process. Helping you to learn to both think more consciously and strengthen your ability to meditate.

This time around I will give you the broad steps, based on what you have done with God, Death and Material Security. You will do the smaller steps yourself. By doing the smaller 'prep work' and refreshing your mind of the process, you will solidify how to use the process that you have worked through three times already. The ultimate goal is for you to be so familiar with the system that you can do it from start to finish…without me, without this book ☺

Step 1: The following statements are a starting point. Be sure to add any others that come to your mind. When adding beliefs, remember that they do not have to be beliefs that you think you hold. Just add any commonly held beliefs that come to mind.

Sexuality Beliefs

1. If we obeyed God's laws regarding sex, sexually transmitted diseases would not exist.

2. Sex is exclusively for procreation.

3. Outside of a sanctioned marriage, sex is a sin.

4. Sexuality and a spiritual path are not compatible.

5. Celibacy or abstinence is required of those who choose to serve God.

6. Children should be taught, encouraged and disciplined to restrain their sexual urges until at least the age of 18 or 20.

7. Sex, simply for pleasure, is ok.

8. Men should 'sow their wild oats' while Women should remain chaste.

9. Women should not wear men's clothing

10. Sexual identity is separate from spiritual identity.

11. Gay and Lesbian sex is against nature's law.

12. Masturbation is the spilling of 'God's seed' and therefore a sin.

13. Tubelligations, birth control pills and vasectomies are 'interfering with nature'.

14. Sexual relationships should be monogamous.

15. Sexual identity is learned.

Step 2: Elaborate and go deeper for each statement with one or two sentences that help convey what is at the root of the common belief. Remember how I did this for you with God and Death? Or, add an opposing belief like I did with the Material Security beliefs. Look back to those for examples of how this may be done.

This part is about understanding the belief, not determining if you hold it. You'll do that with your daily exercises and ponderings. I have started you off with numbers 6 and 10, using an opposing beliefs example and then an elaboration.

6. Children should be taught, encouraged and disciplined to restrain their sexual urges until at least the age of 18 or 20. **Children should be allowed to explore their sexuality whenever they start to become curious**

10. Sexual identity is separate from spiritual identity.

    Many religious and spiritual teachings advocate suppressing sexual identity and action. Some of these teachings take the guise of putting forth that sexual energy is a lower energy, a base energy, and a hindrance to spiritual enlightenment. Other teachings allow sexuality and even sex but only under certain conditions…marriage, procreation, etc.

No need to turn the page until you have worked through and completed you elaborations and opposing beliefs ☺.

Step 3: Reread pages 118-122, the daily meditative exercises that you used for both God and Death. Use those exercises now with the common beliefs about sexuality.

Much like what occurred when you looked at the previous FBS, when you start to look closer, you may indeed find that you hold a belief that on the surface you initially said, "No, not me." You define ourselves as much by what you don't believe as by what you do ☺

No need to go to the next page for at least 7 or 8 days. You should be back at pages 118-122 ☺

Step 4: Create a list like on page 137, use one or two words to identify each belief and then fill in what experiences YOUR beliefs about Sexuality create in your life. What type of experience picture emerges?

1.
2.
3
4.
5.
6.
7.
8.
9.
10.
11.
12.
13.
14.
15.

Don't rush. Remember to meditate, contemplate and look through your life to see what is true about your experience.

Step 5: Now create your negative/positive columned sheet and list your belief experiences from Step 4. As before, take a few days to ponder what is revealed now.

Positive   Negative

Or, instead of Negative and Positive maybe name the columns 'What I want' and 'What I Don't Want'. Remember, this is about understanding what EXEPRIENCES your beliefs create.

Step 6: Choose two of your beliefs, the experiences of which you'd like to change, and map out a seven step approach to changing them similar to the process you followed for God on pages 139-144 and Death on pages 158-161.

Sexuality, of the four FBS, involves other people in it's own unique way. Propelling us towards some people and pushing us away from others. It is also the one that we use as a hammer to judge very heavily with. And in many respects, this FBS may sometimes interfere with the most important relationship in each of your lives; our relationship with our God. Interestingly, it is what we believe, or have been taught that God believes, about sexuality and gender, that causes us the most trouble. Hopefully, you now have a head start on having a sexuality that enhances your life rather than hinders it.

A Tailor's Dummy

"Believe nothing, no matter where you read it, or who said it, no matter if I have said it, unless it agrees with your own reason and your own common sense." Buddha

The wisdom in the quote above is worth living by. You have considered, explored and meditated on things of great importance. My goal throughout has been to provide a practical framework by which you could discover and explore your own beliefs and experiences. I have taken great care to be sure to encourage you to draw your own conclusions and have your own experiences, not mine.

I imagine this frame work to be much like a tailor's dummy. The frame does not dictate the tailors work. It simply supports and allows the creation to take place with the proper support. A tailor can hang any type of fabric on the dummy and create any style of clothing, for both men and women. He can incorporate zippers, buttons or buckles.

The ideas and concepts and the tools and exercises that have been presented here are a suggested framework for a meditation practice and for exploring your Beliefs. You may use it to explore, enhance and change your experience of yourself and life. And like a tailors dummy, this frame work is adjustable and customizable to your needs.

As you can see from all of the hard work that you have done thus far, you are an amazing and complex being with many facets that reveal the powerful creative Being that you are. I said early-on 'there is so much more at play then what we would look at through these pages.' And there is.

You looked at the creative nature of your thoughts and Beliefs Systems. And you used an amazing tool to do this....your mind. You implemented a meditation practice to help you understand how to more effectively use that tool.

What you have done here can be put into perspective by using space exploration as a comparison. You've become acquainted with the gear and technology that will support and power your journey, anywhere you set your sights on. You've prepared for the mission by exploring your Foundational Belief Systems. And you've now come out onto the launch-pad.

The further journey may be some aspects of your creative nature that we did not specifically touch on during your trip to the launch-pad including Fate, Destiny, Co-Creation, Intuition and Choice. Mentioning these here is to remind you to be fully aware that you are more than your thoughts. You are complex and amazing and the elements that come together to create you and your experience of life are numerous.

I used to say that the ideas and practices that I have written about here changed my life. That is not true. I changed my life by using these ideas and practices. And by also being willing and open to changing them, adding to them and even dropping some of them along the way. What worked 10 years ago may not work now. What didn't work two weeks ago may work now. I invite you to approach life in this same way. By doing so you will discover that the answers that you seek are always within grasp when your mind and heart are open.

Onward

This final chapter contains a short list of some of the tools and exercises that have been suggested throughout the book. I wanted to list some of them in one, easy to find place. Please use them often, change and add to them and create your own.

1. Thoughts create matter. Every human made thing was at first a thought in someone's mind.
    EVERYTHING.
2. Thoughts attract circumstances, people and states of being into your life that have similar qualities as those same thoughts.
3. Thoughts form beliefs, which determine how you experience everything. What you believe about something is how you experience it.

My practical definition of meditation is 'giving your mind a task rather than letting it give you the task.'

- Meditation is simple, but not always easy
- Practice daily
- Turn off your TV for the first 30 days
- Limit your computer time to just the necessary things.
- Be conscious of your breath throughout the day
- Join a meditation group or find a friend who would like to meditate together once a week
- View this as fun and exciting (because it is)

BREATHING correctly and consciously is essential to any meditation practice. Breathing correctly is using your diaphragm to pull your breath down deep into to your lungs, filling them fully. Placing a hand on your chest will help you to be aware if you are chest or diaphragm breathing. You want to have minimal movement in your chest, having your stomach poke out as your breath makes it deep into your lungs.

Exercises

- Stretching The Experience Out
- Recognize when you are Labeling
- Meditate in unusual places
- Talking to your Mind
- 10 minutes, eyes closed, breathing
- 15 minutes, eyes closed, breathing
- 15 minutes, counting backwards
- I Spy your surroundings
- Sticker on 3rd Eye
- Use your Town Center
- 15 minute breathing meditation with a mantra
- 15-minute meditation, say 'WHY' on each exhale.
- Pendulum Exercise
- A No Money Week

Ronald L. Hays

Author's Bio, Workshops and Contact Information

A passion for meditation and understanding how Beliefs create experience and helping people to become empowered through these ideas is the driving force in Ronald's life. After years of teaching and listening, he has come to know and believe that there is nothing new. But, like a sunset viewed by a group of friends, Truth is seen by each person from an intimate and unique perspective; making it new each time.

Ronald offers several types of meditative experiences and workshops in addition to individual meditative experiences.

Signature Crystal Bowl Meditative EXPERIENCE

This 1 hr EXPERIENCE is centered around the Crystal Singing Bowls and the exploration of the creative nature of thoughts. With a mixture of demonstrations, humor, experimentation and practical application, participants will begin to expand their awareness of self, others and the greater whole. No matter where someone considers herself to be in terms of a meditative practice --- from novice to avid practitioner -- the Crystal Bowl Meditative EXPERIENCE will offer a unique way to develop a meditation practice or expound on an existing practice. Each month you will be given a new tool and exercise to build upon and further strengthen your ability to get beneath the chatter of you mind.

Foundational Belief Systems Experiential Workshop

Through a regular meditation practice you can delve into what Ronald calls Foundational Belief Systems (FBS), of which there are four: God, Death, Material Security and Sexuality. A thorough understanding of what you believe in these areas and how those beliefs are creating ALL of your life experiences will bring you a new awareness that can transform your life---if you choose. During the workshop, you will explore meditation---what, how, when, where—not only with the amazing Quartz Crystal Singing Bowls but with practical techniques and exercises that will allow you to take the experience with you into your daily routine. You will use these to take a closer look at one of your own Foundational Belief Systems. Ronald's mixture of analogy and humor along with practical suggestions, tools, and exercises come together to provide you with a firm basis for exploring fully the creative nature of your thoughts and the FBS that they create.

The workshop is only the beginning.........

12 Principles/12 Meditations EXPERIENCE

This series of meditations is built around the principles that anchor all 12 Step Programs. No particular 12 Step Program will be discussed--only the principles. So whether someone is in AA, NA, SA, OA or no "A" they are welcome to join and explore and meditate on these powerful principles.

Week #1 Surrender

Week #2 Hope

Week #3 Commitment

Week #4 Honesty

Week #5 Truth

Week #6 Willingness

Week #7 Humility

Week#8 Reflection

Week #9 Amendment

Week #10 Vigilance

Week #11 Attunement

Week #12 Service

The first 15 minutes is devoted to a brief introduction of that week's principle followed by a ½ hr Crystal Bowl Meditation. The last 15 minutes will be for group sharing and contemplation of the principle from a meditative state and how to explore it over the coming week.

For more information, to sign up for a workshop or
meditative experience and to contact Ronald please visit
www.theglobalpage.com

Additional copies of *You Believe, You Experience* may be
purchased individually or at wholesale pricing, for authorized
resellers, at www.theglobalpage.com and www.amazon.com